Maarten Sleeuwits
Objects and Recordings

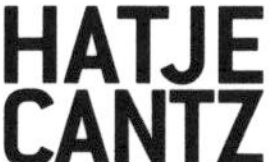

Chocolate, 2009
Aluminiumfolie, Bambus und bemalter Karton

Dieses Objekt wurde so gefertigt, dass es in meine
Manteltasche passt. Das Werk macht ein knisterndes
Geräusch, sobald man es bewegt.

Chocolate, 2009
Aluminum foil, bamboo, and painted cardboard

This object is made to fit into the pocket of my
coat. The work produces a crackling sound when
set in motion.

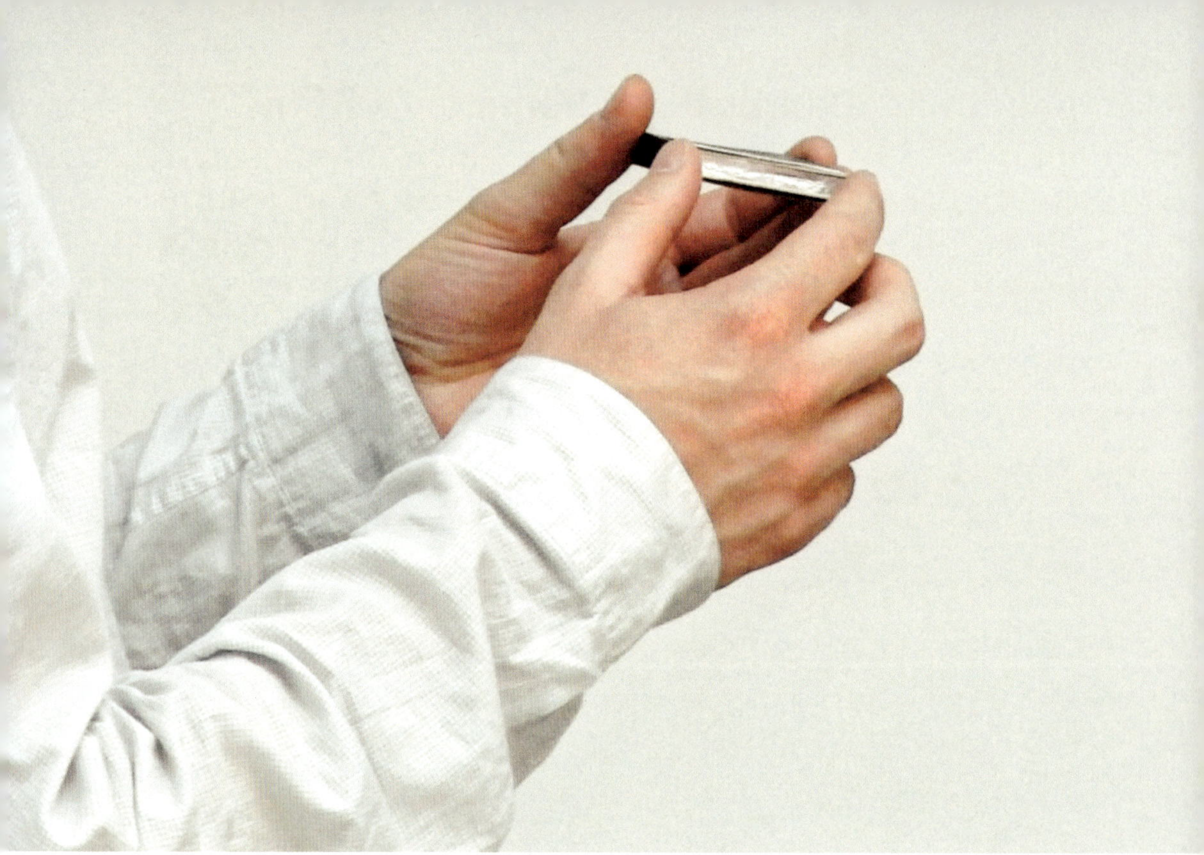

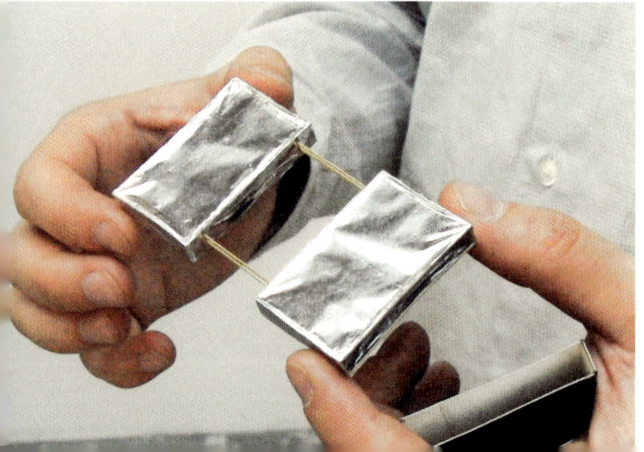

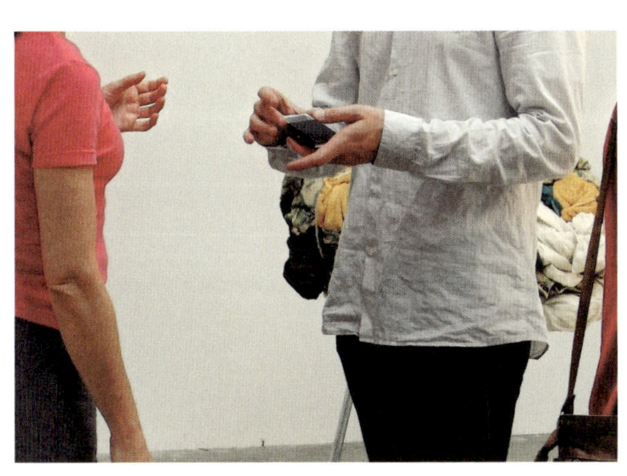

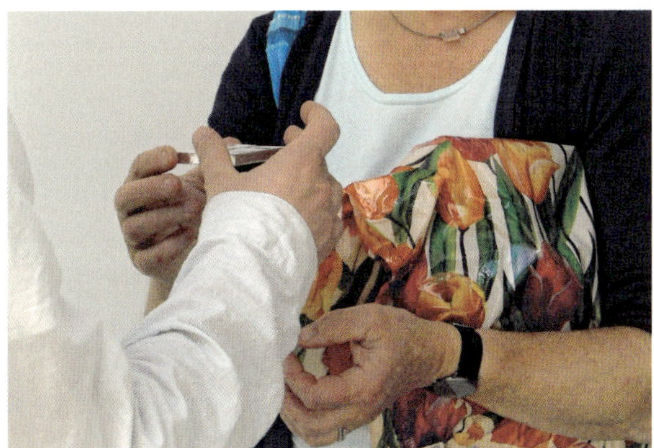

X, 2010
Blei

Dieses Objekt wurde von vier Männern getragen.

X, 2010
Lead

This object was carried by four men.

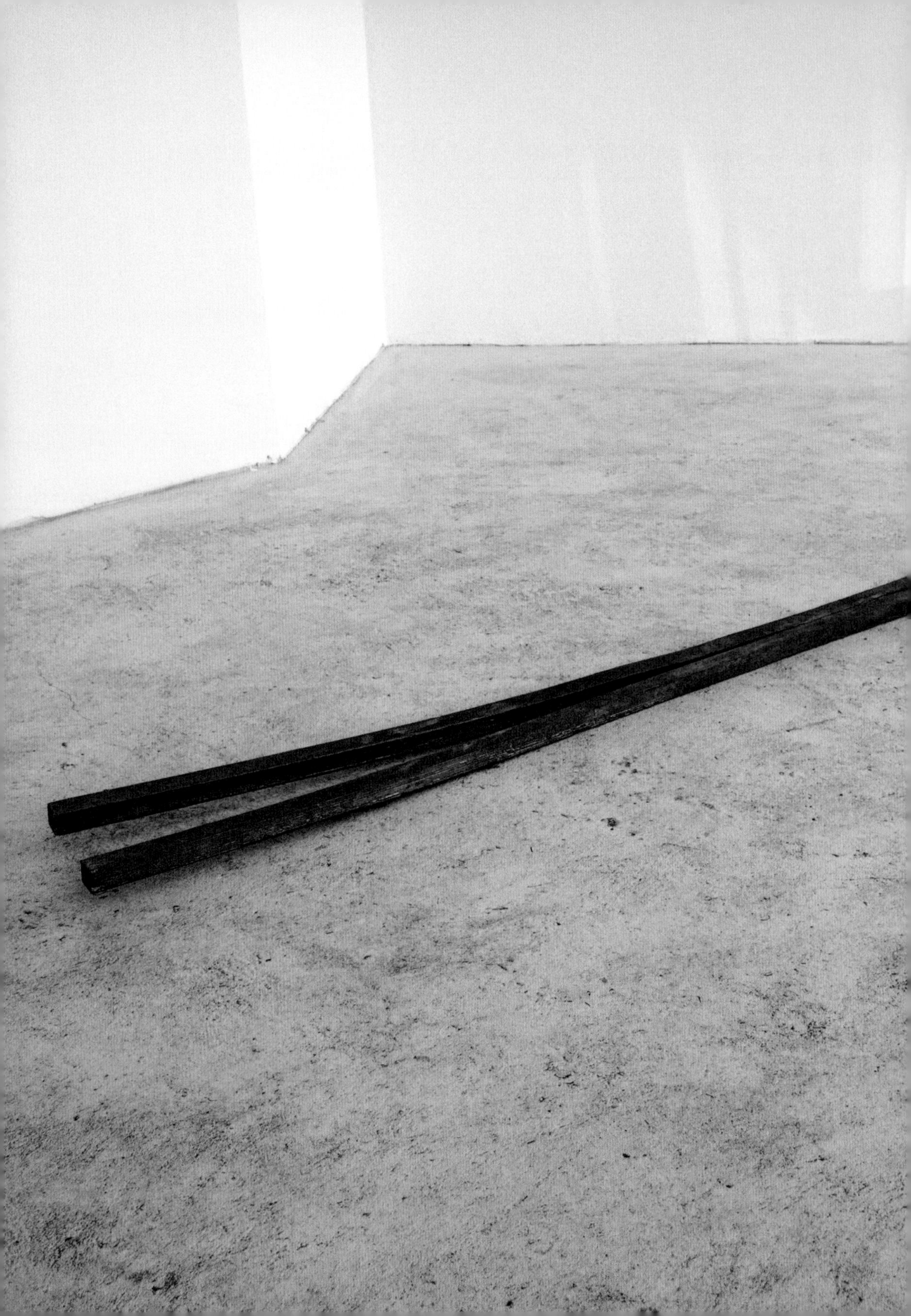

Zero, 2005—2010
Technische Keramik und 24 Karat Gold

Die Form dieses kleinen, besonders schweren
Quaders lässt sich durch Fingerdruck verändern.

Zero, 2005—2010
Technical ceramics and twenty-four-carat gold

The shape of this small, extraordinarily heavy
cuboid can be altered by applying pressure
with one's fingers.

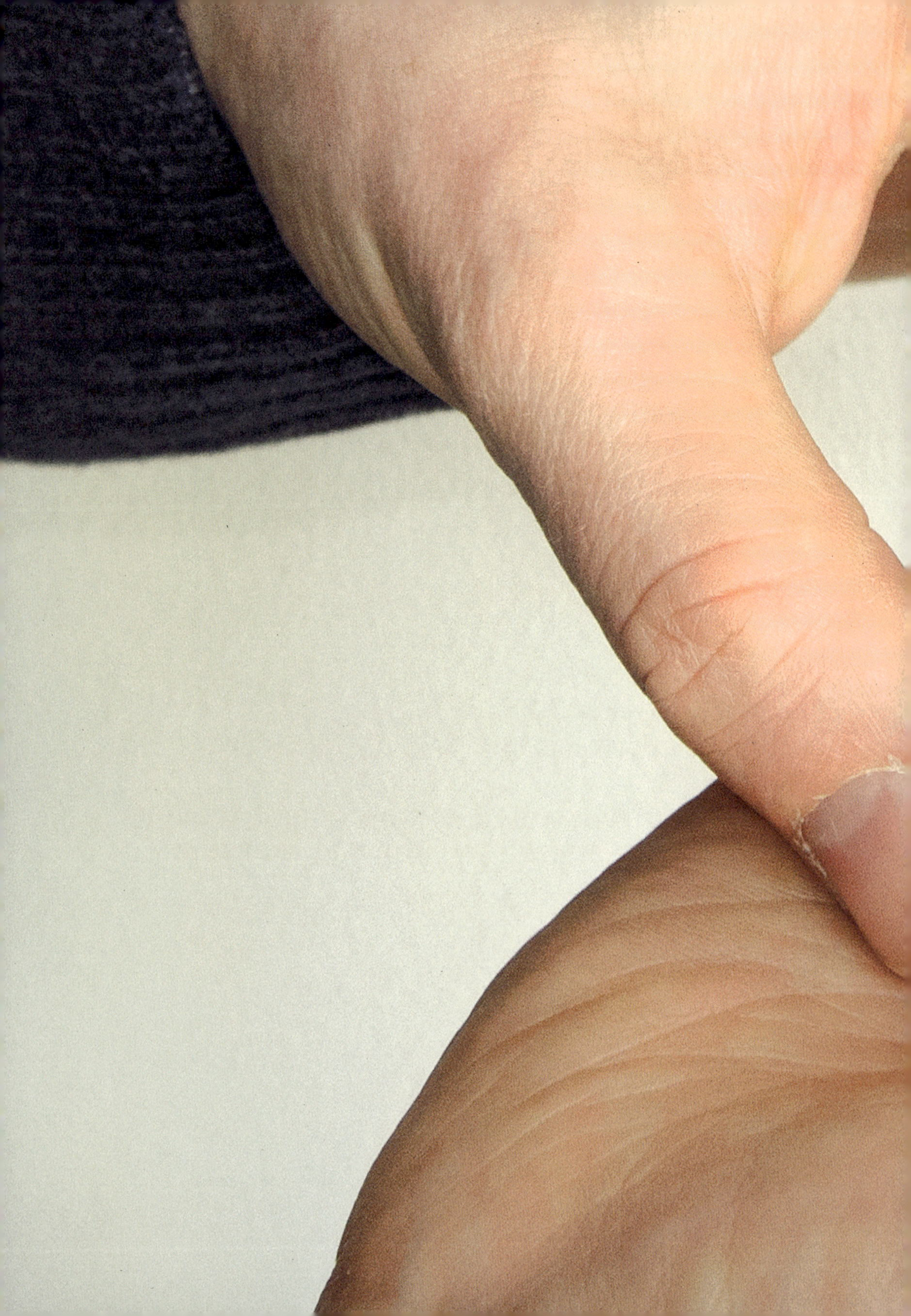

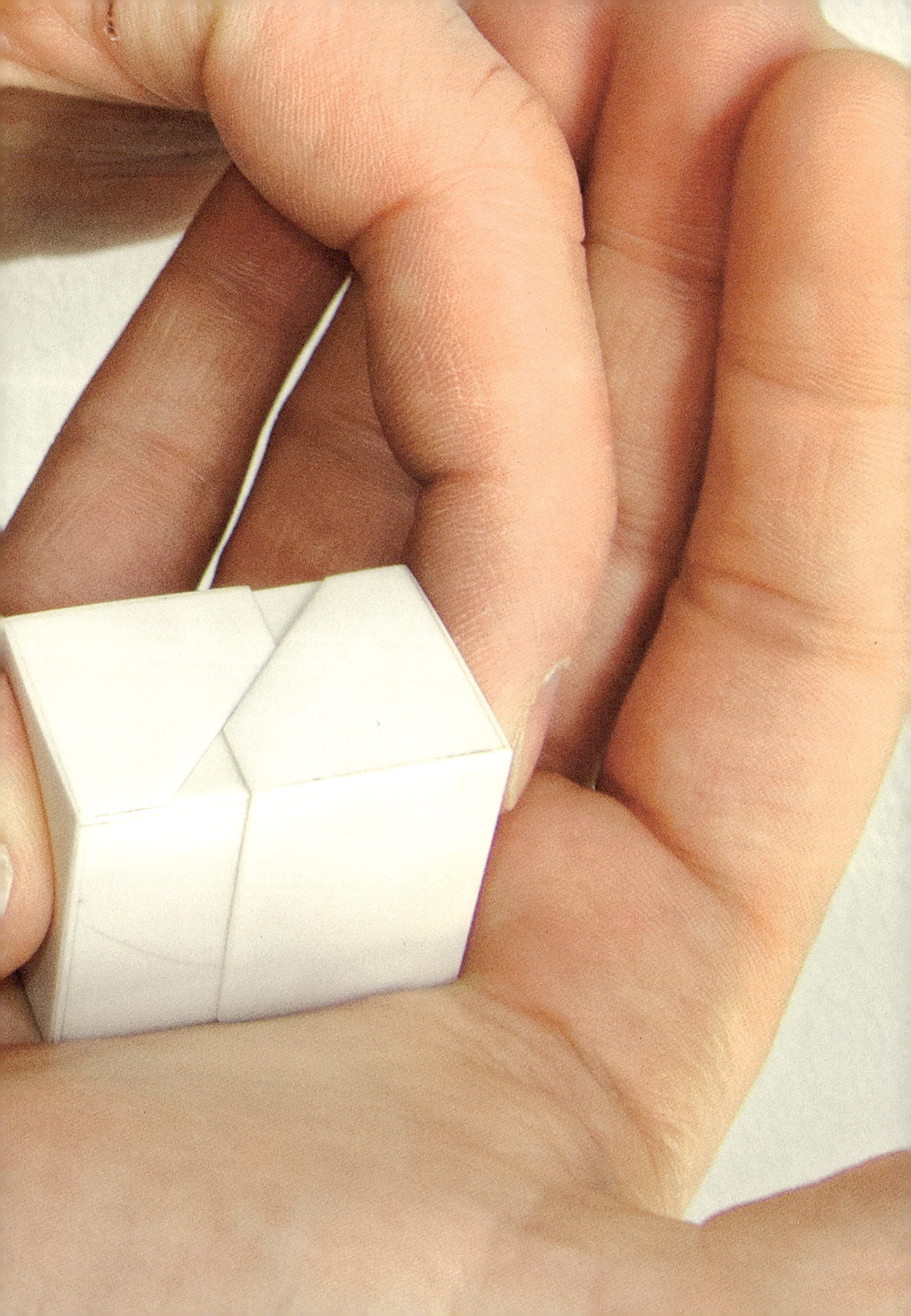

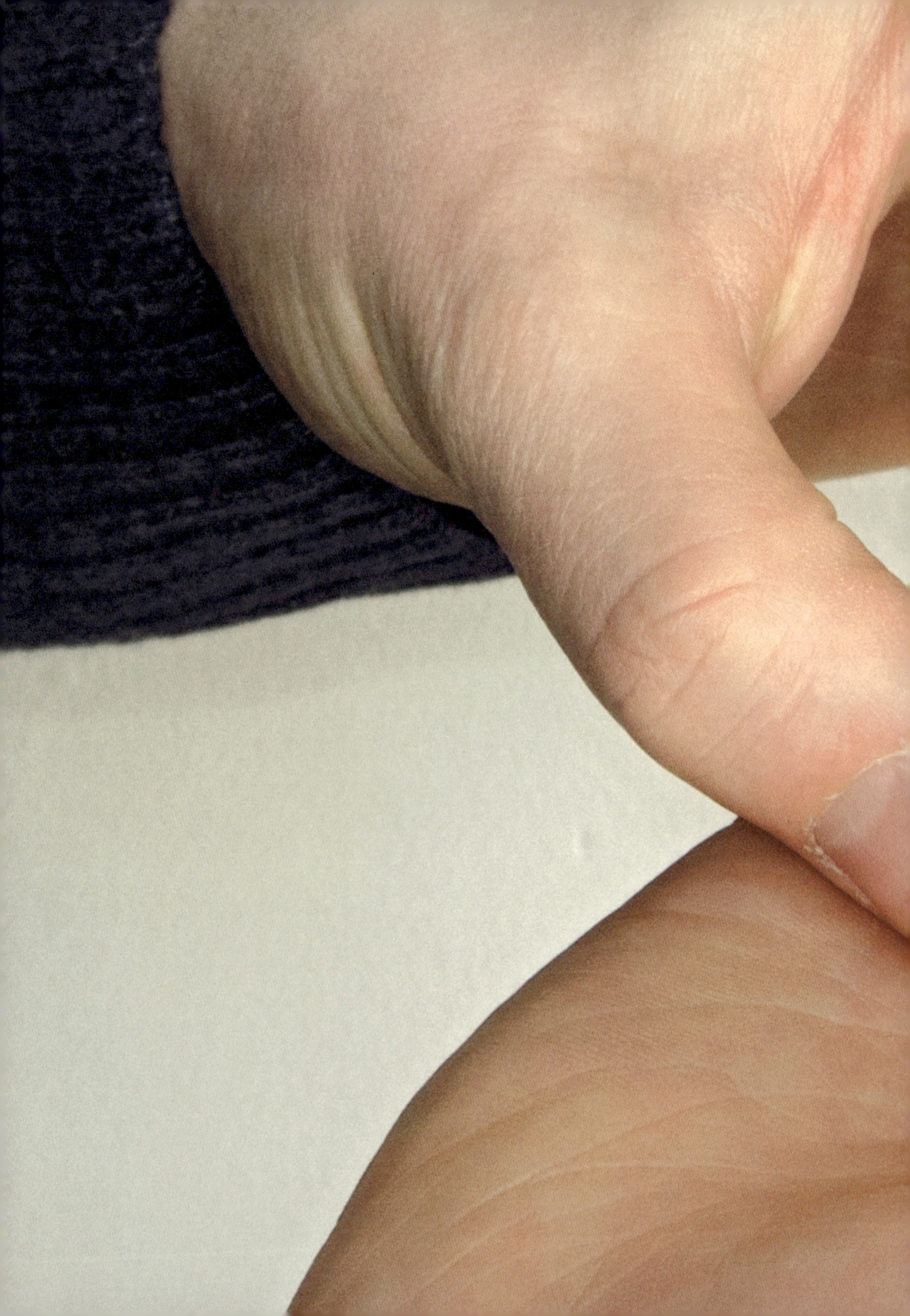

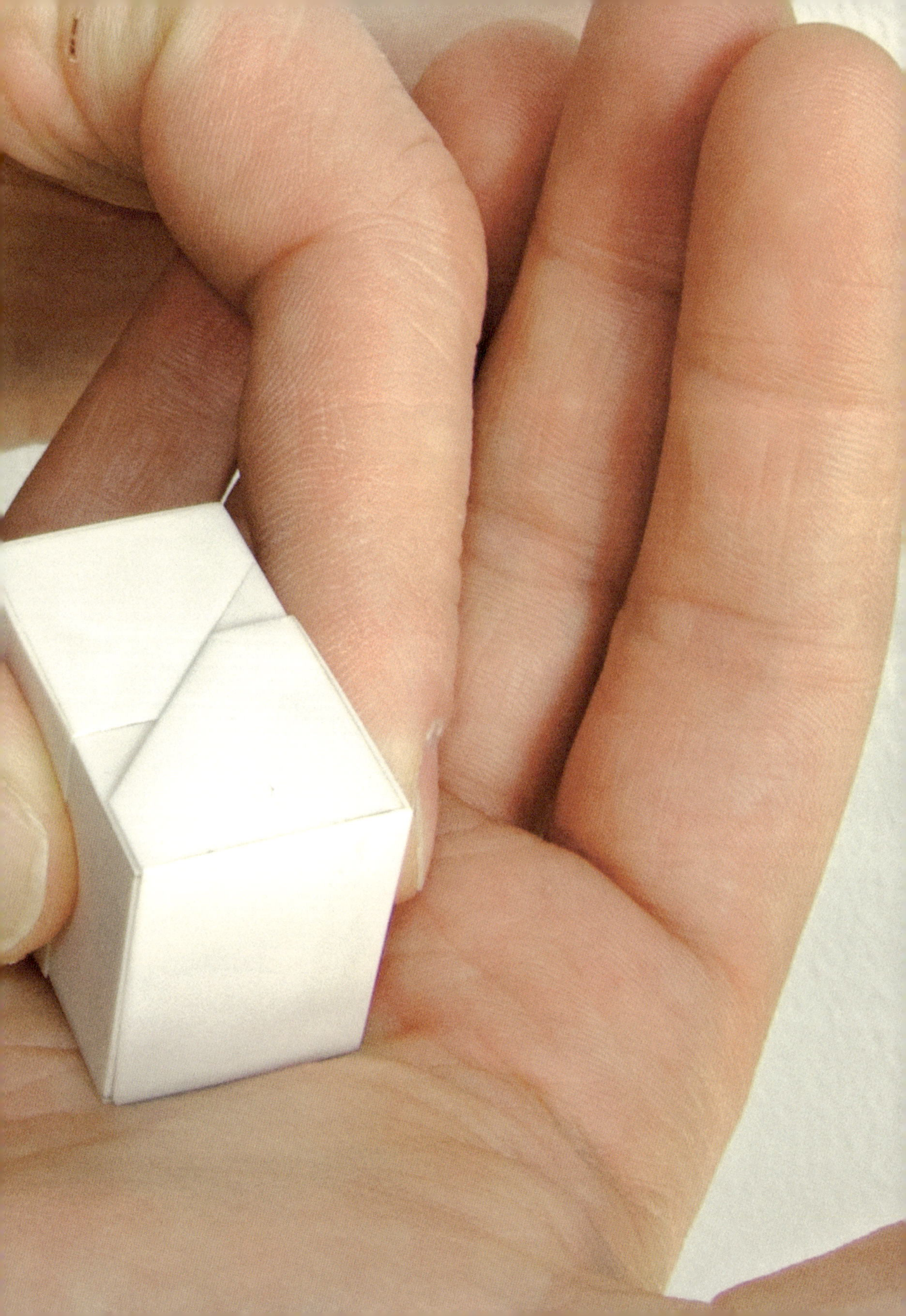

I Asked the Japanese Artist Lei Saito What
Would Be the Best Method for Wrapping
a Piece of Silk around My Work Zero So
the Object Would Be Well Protected in Its
Box, 2010
Tintenstrahldruck auf Fotopapier

Die Bilder dieses 94-seitigen Daumenkinos zeigen,
wie man das Werk Zero in seine Schachtel packt.

I Asked the Japanese Artist Lei Saito What
Would Be the Best Method for Wrapping
a Piece of Silk around My Work Zero So
the Object Would Be Well Protected in Its
Box, 2010
Ink-jet print on photo paper

These images, taken from a ninety-four-page flip-
book, show how to put the work Zero in its box.

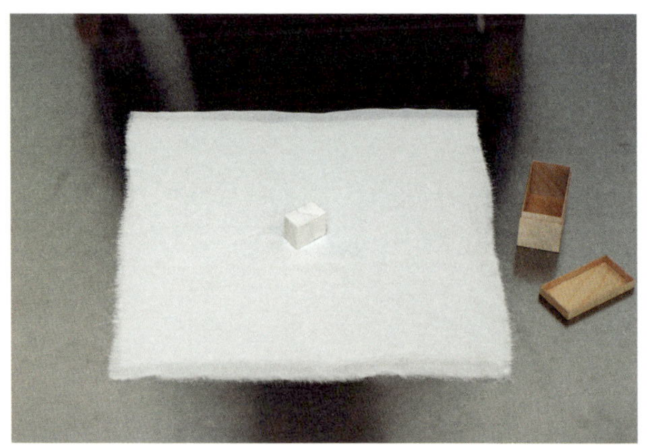

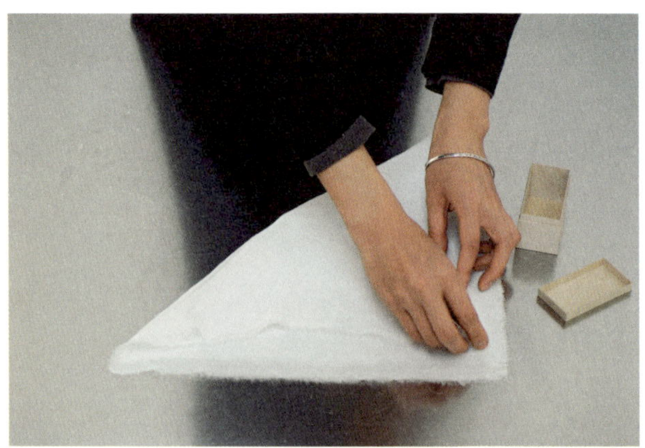

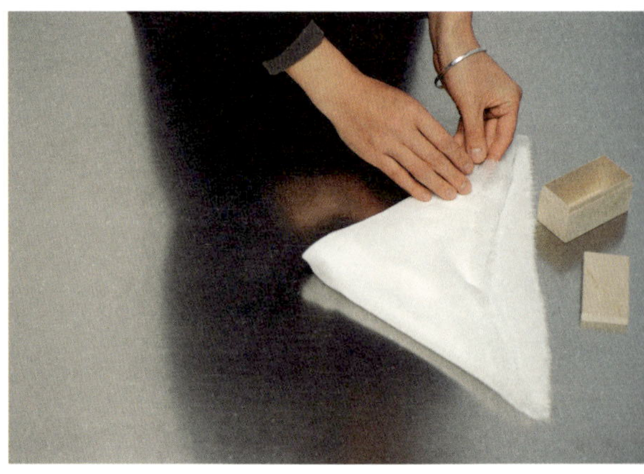

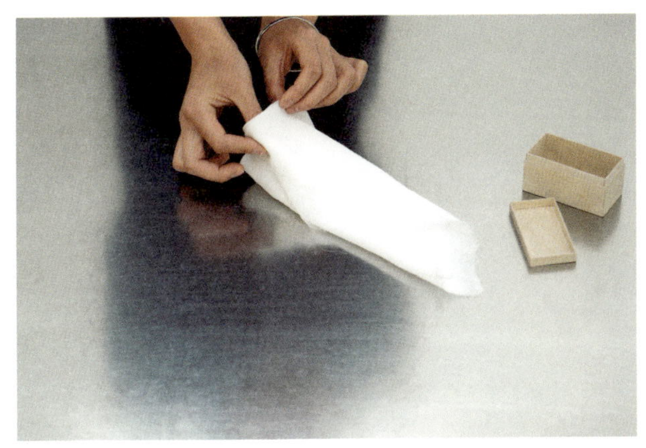

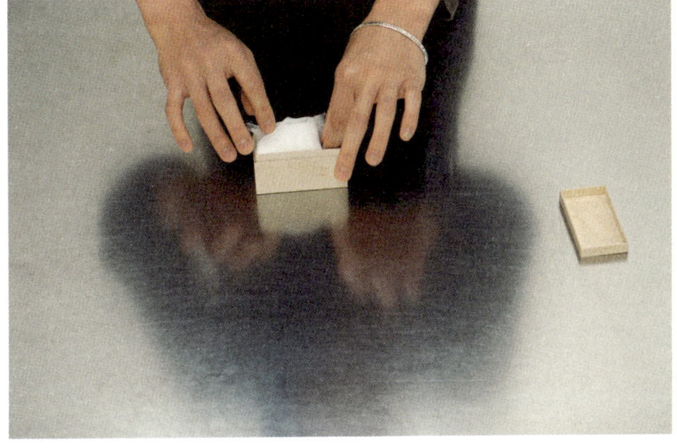

A Satellite to Send Away, 2009
Bambus, Karton, Anleitung und ein Briefumschlag

Dieses Objekt passt in einen kleinen Briefumschlag und soll nach speziellen Vorgaben weiterversendet werden.

A Satellite to Send Away, 2009
Bamboo, cardboard box, instruction card and an envelope

This object is made to fit into a small envelope and has to be exchanged by mail according to specific instructions.

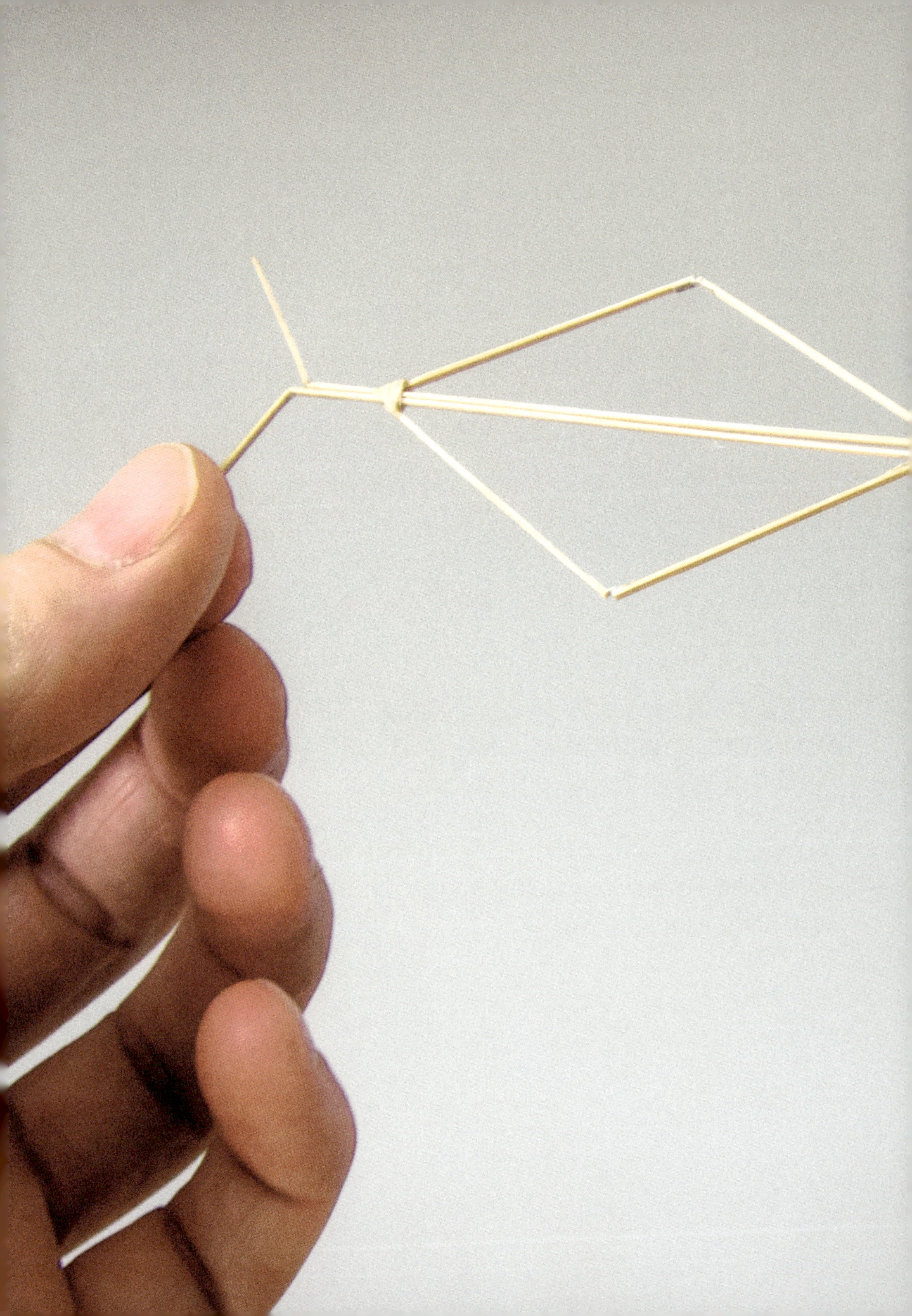

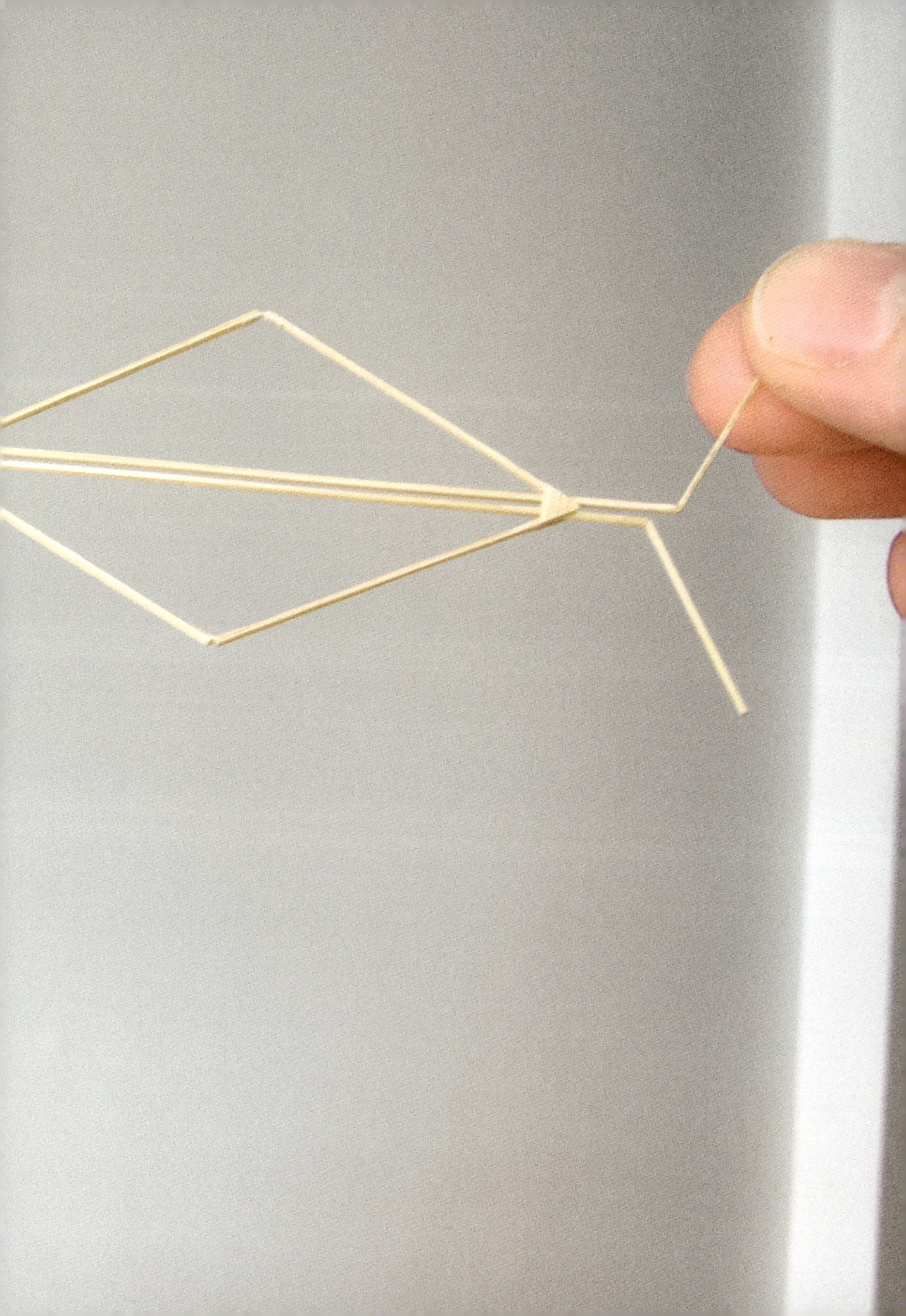

Moving Bone China, 2010
Porzellan

Dieses zerbrechliche Objekt macht Geräusche,
sobald man es bewegt.

Moving Bone China, 2010
Porcelain

This fragile porcelain object produces sounds when
set in motion.

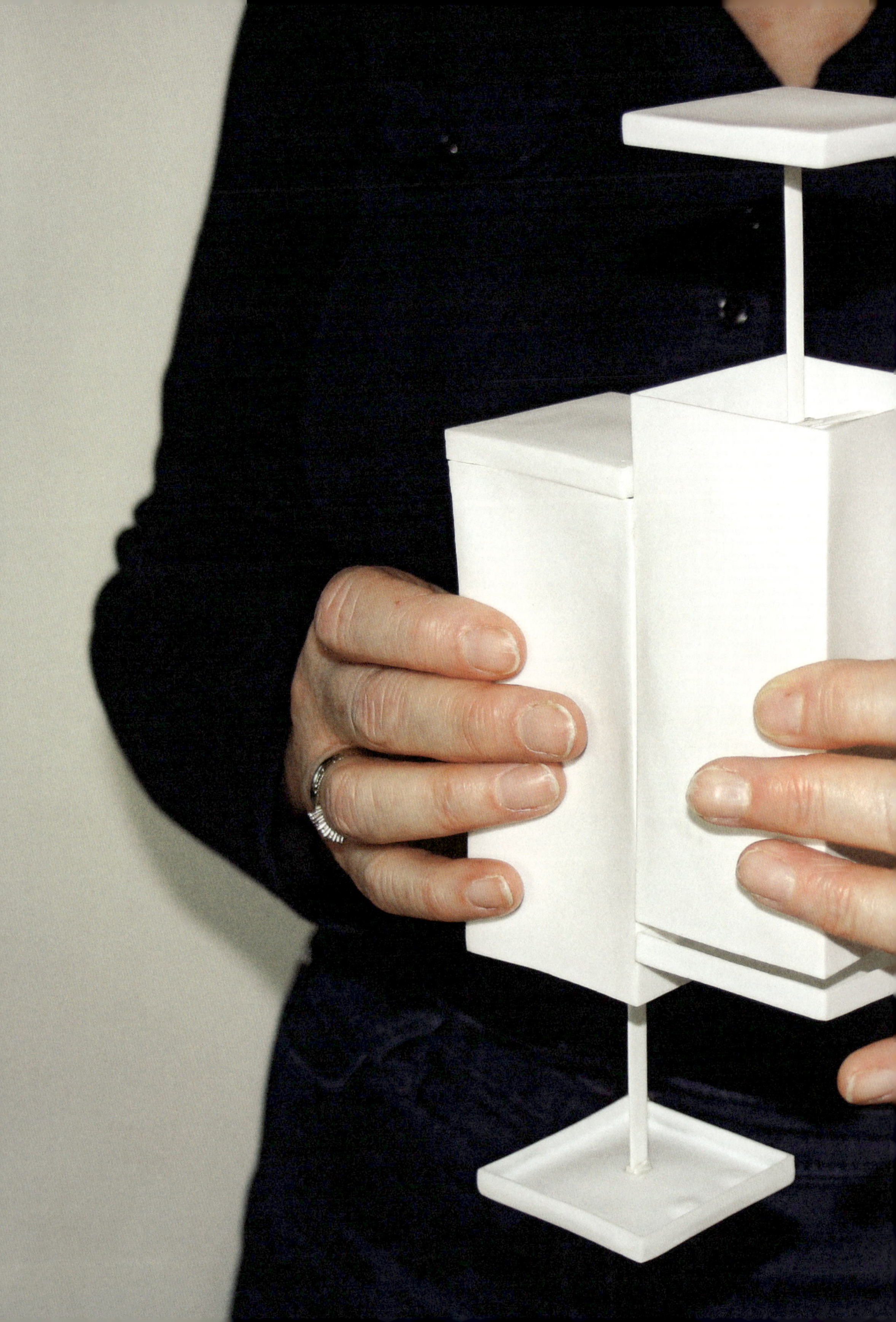

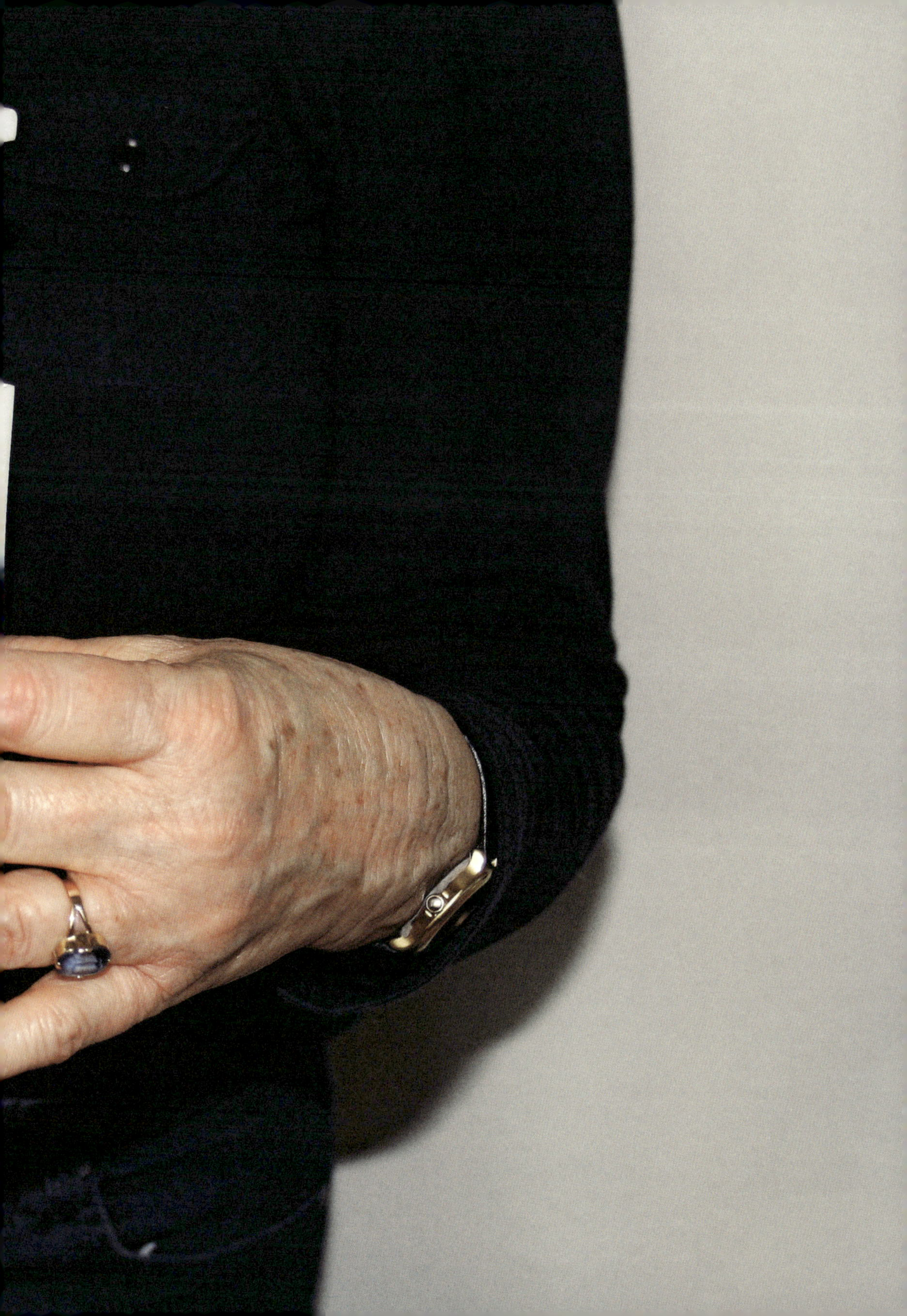

Rome, Summer 2011, 2011
Papiertüte und Sekundenkleber

Während einer zweiwöchigen Studienreise
nach Rom habe ich diese Papiertüte regelmäßig
verwendet und repariert.

Rome, Summer 2011, 2011
Paper bag and superglue

I continuously used and repaired this paper bag
during a two-week study trip to Rome.

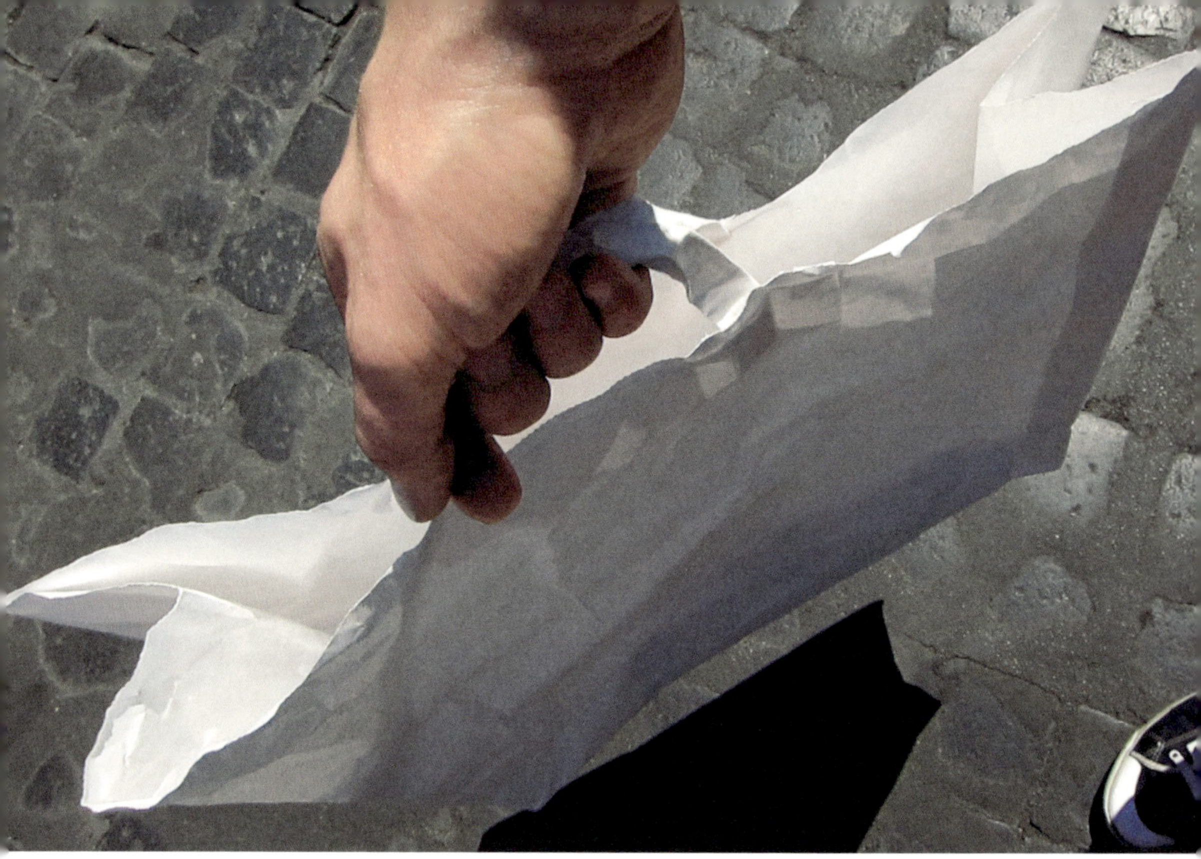

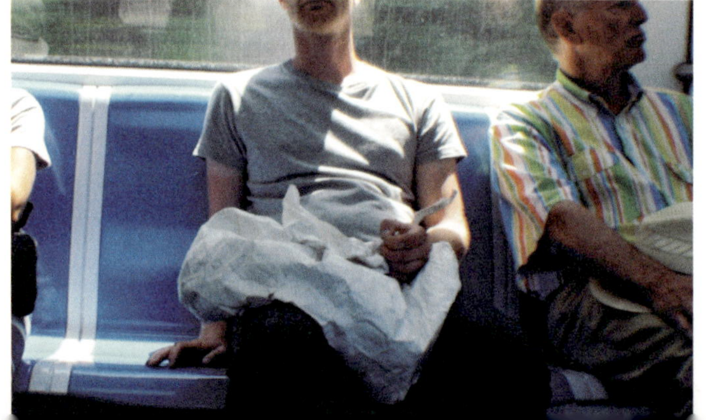

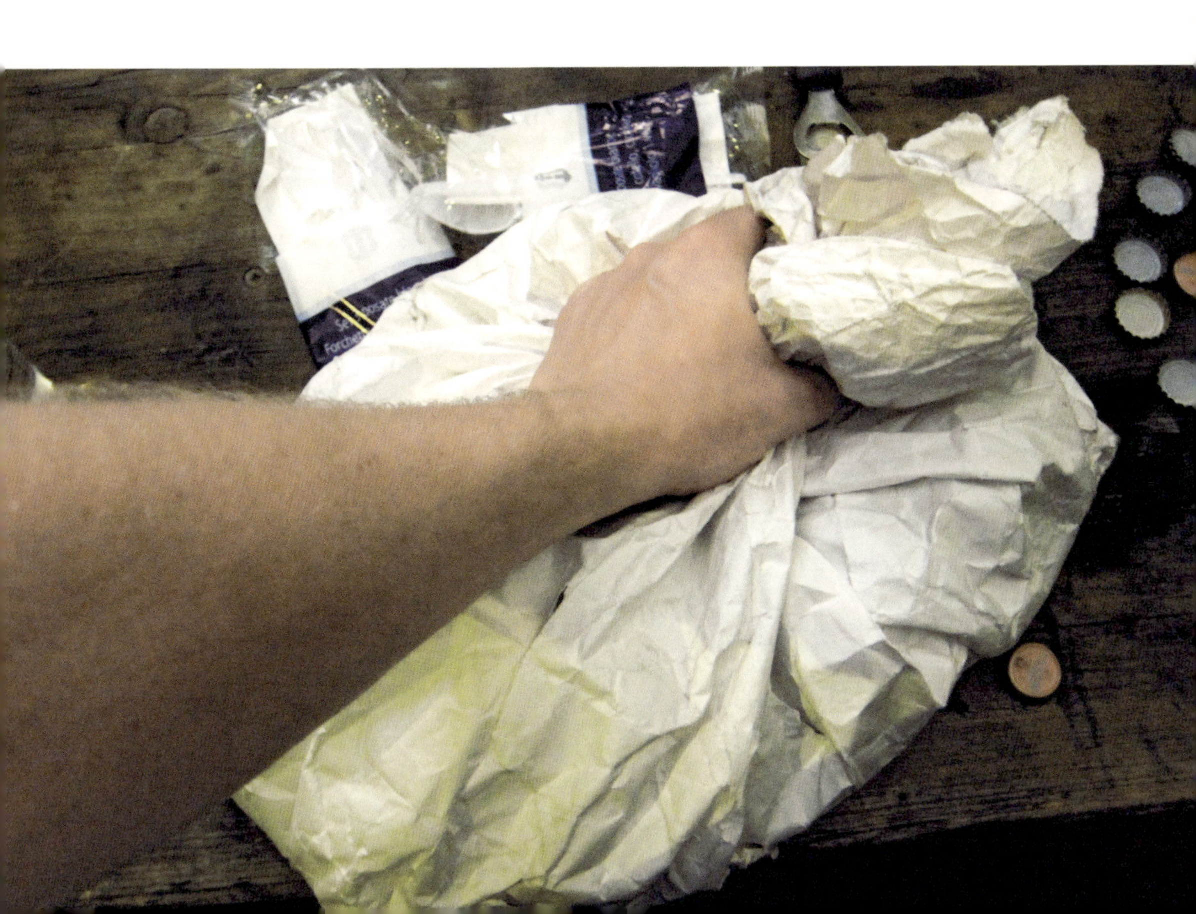

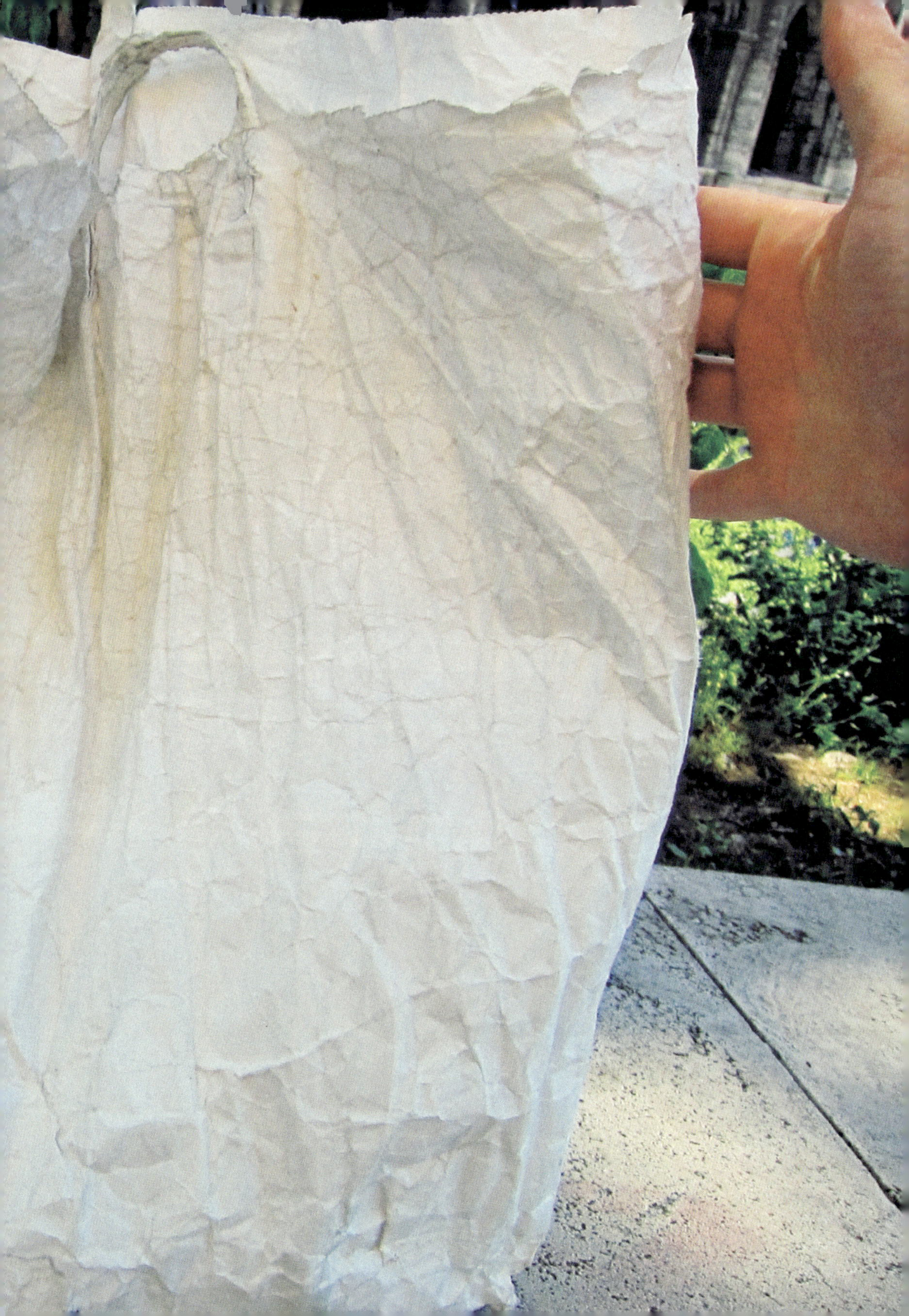

Plumbum, 2010
Blei

Diese Schneideschablone für Porzellanteile
ist zu einem eigenständigen Werk geworden.

Plumbum, 2010
Lead

This cutting template for porcelain parts became
a work in its own right.

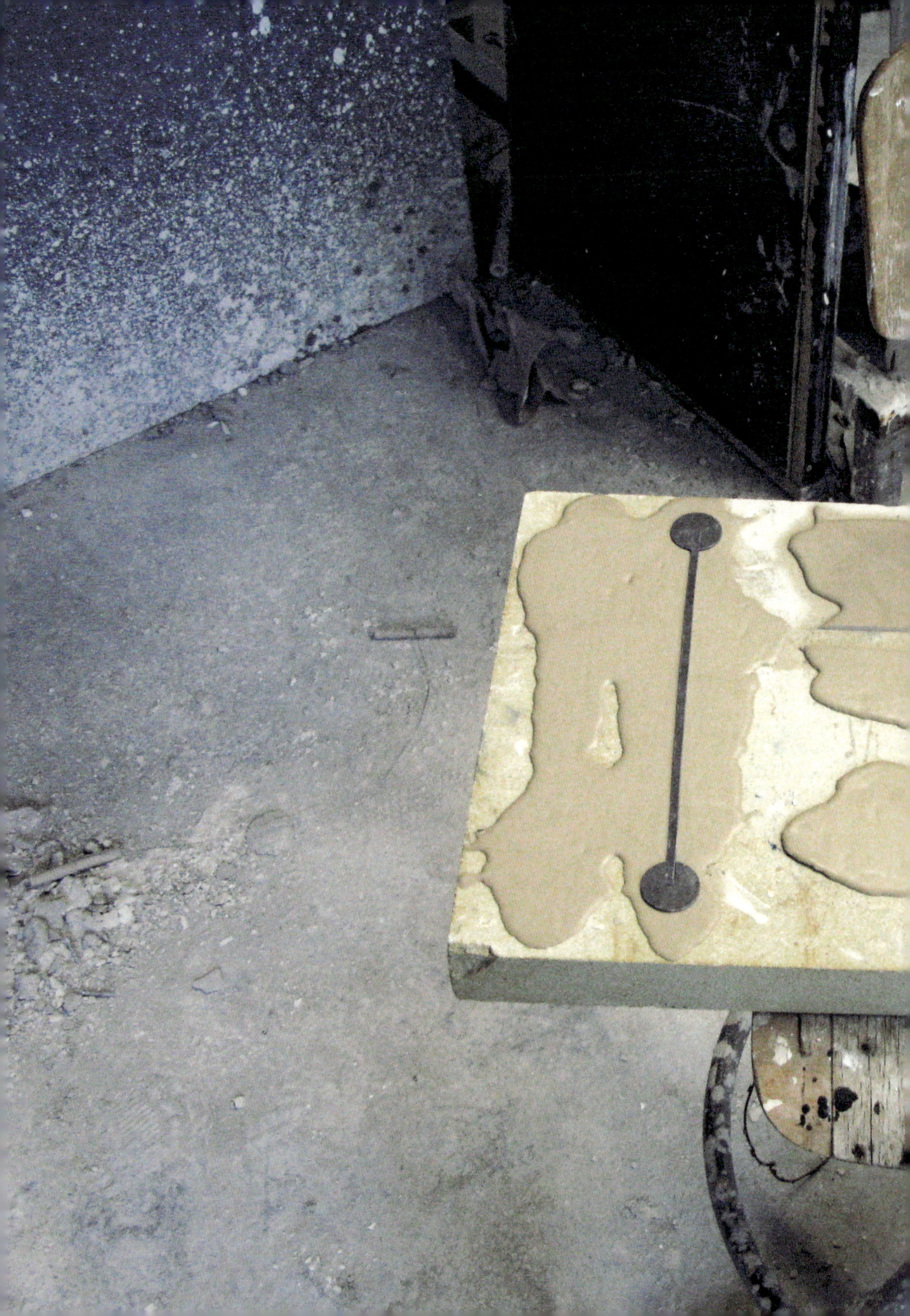

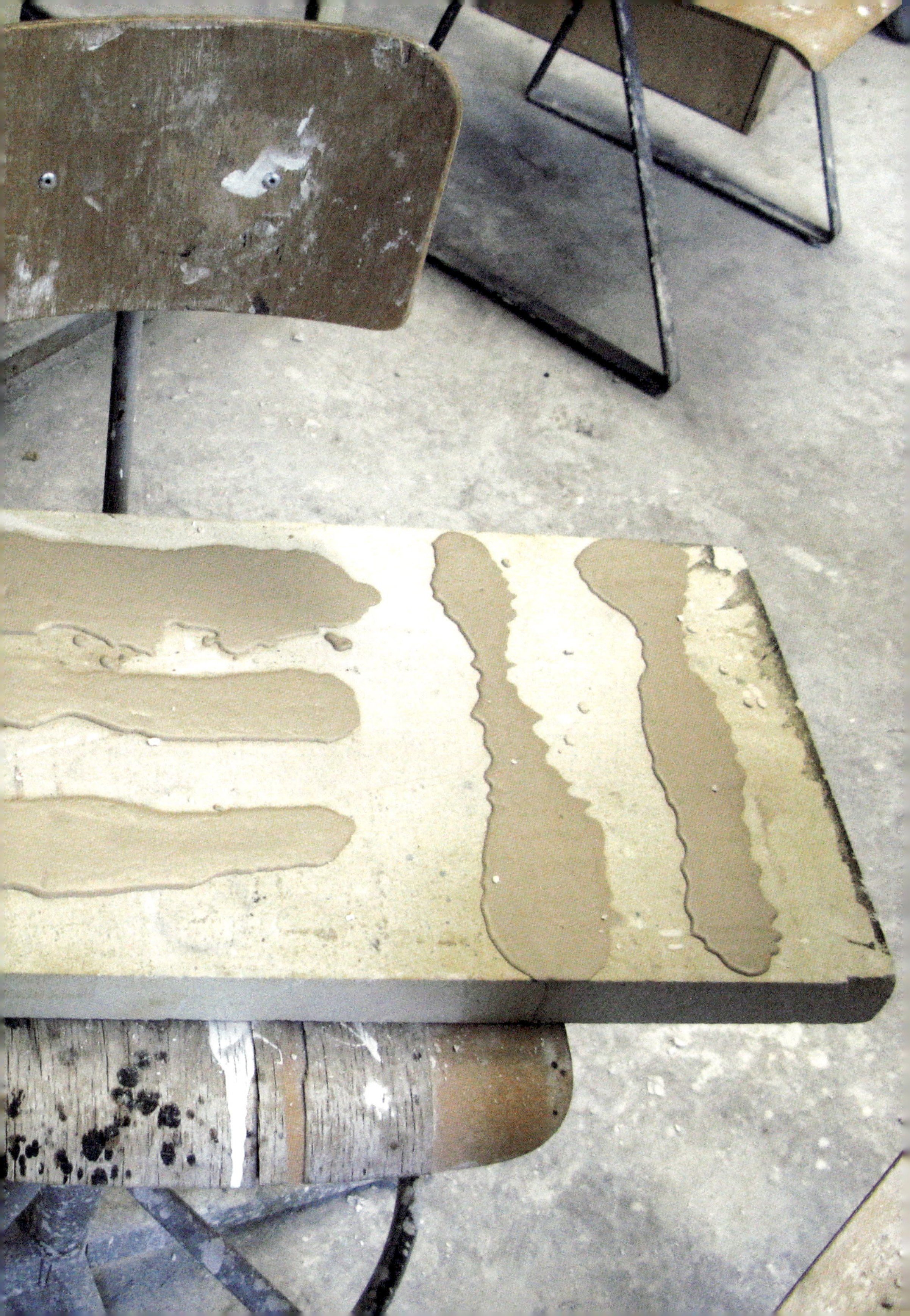

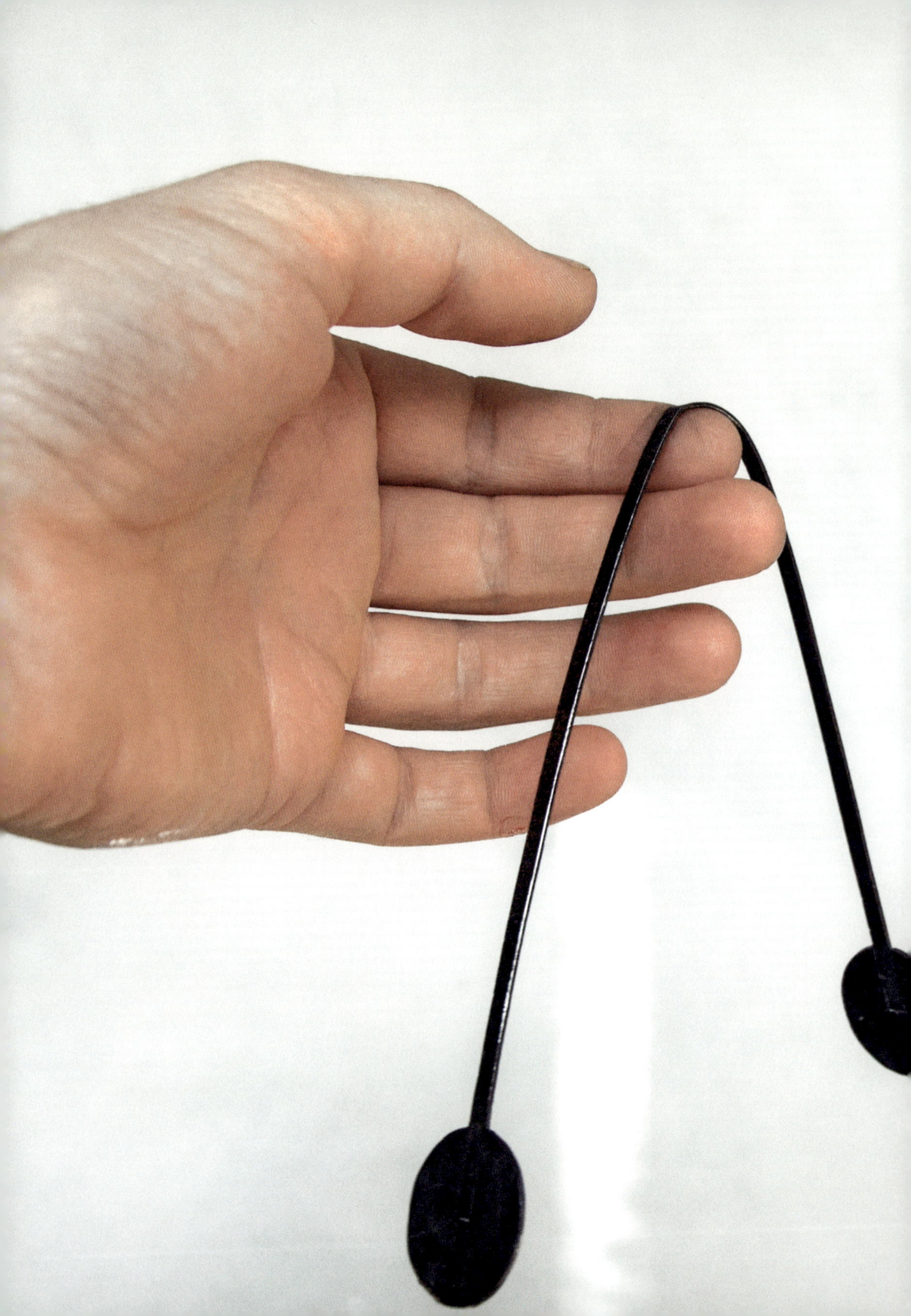

Recording No. 2, 2011
Weißer Ton

135 Kilogramm Ton wurden zu einer 9,5 Meter langen
»Schlange« geformt und von vierzehn Personen
aus der Werkstatt zum Ausstellungsraum getragen.

Recording No. 2, 2011
White clay

135 kilograms of clay were extruded to a 9.5-meter-
long roll and carried by fourteen people from the
site of production to the exhibition space.

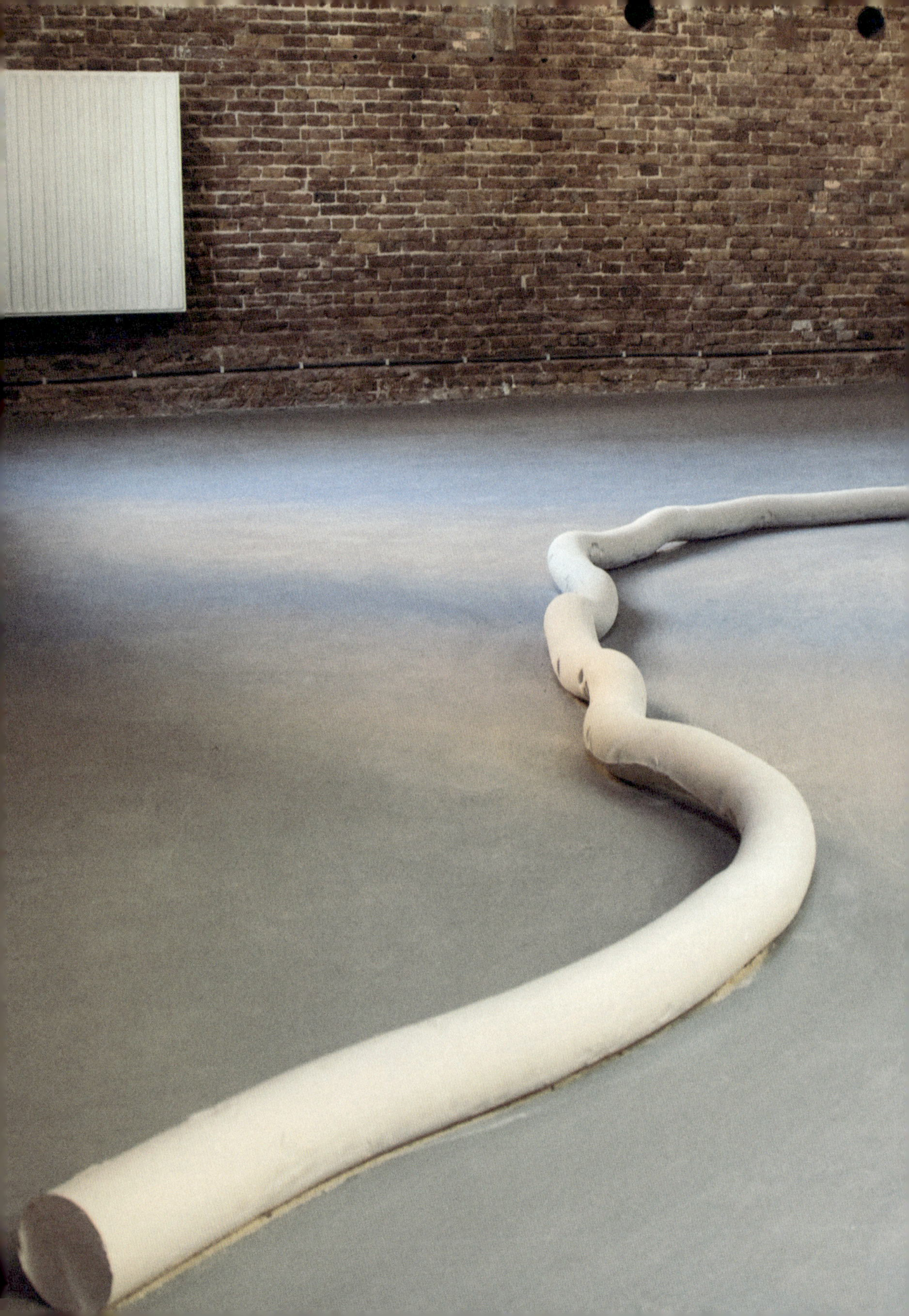

Recording No. 2 (Map), 2012
Digitaldruck auf ungestrichenem Papier, geklebt

Dies ist eine 9,5 Meter lange fotografische
Dokumentation von Recording No. 2 (Ausschnitt).

Recording No. 2 (Map), 2012
Digital print on uncoated paper, glued

This is a 9.5-meter-long photographic documentation
of Recording No. 2 (detail).

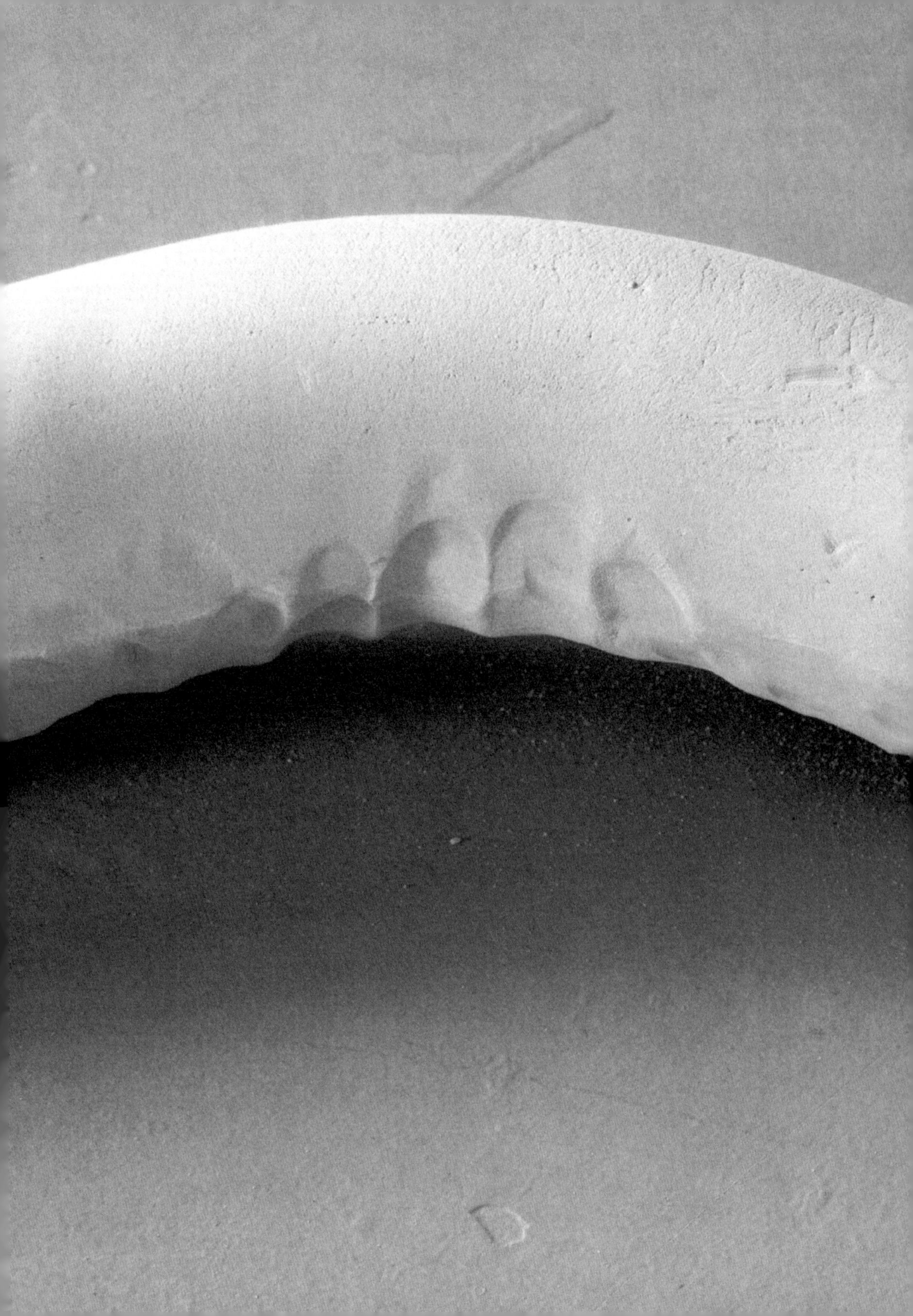

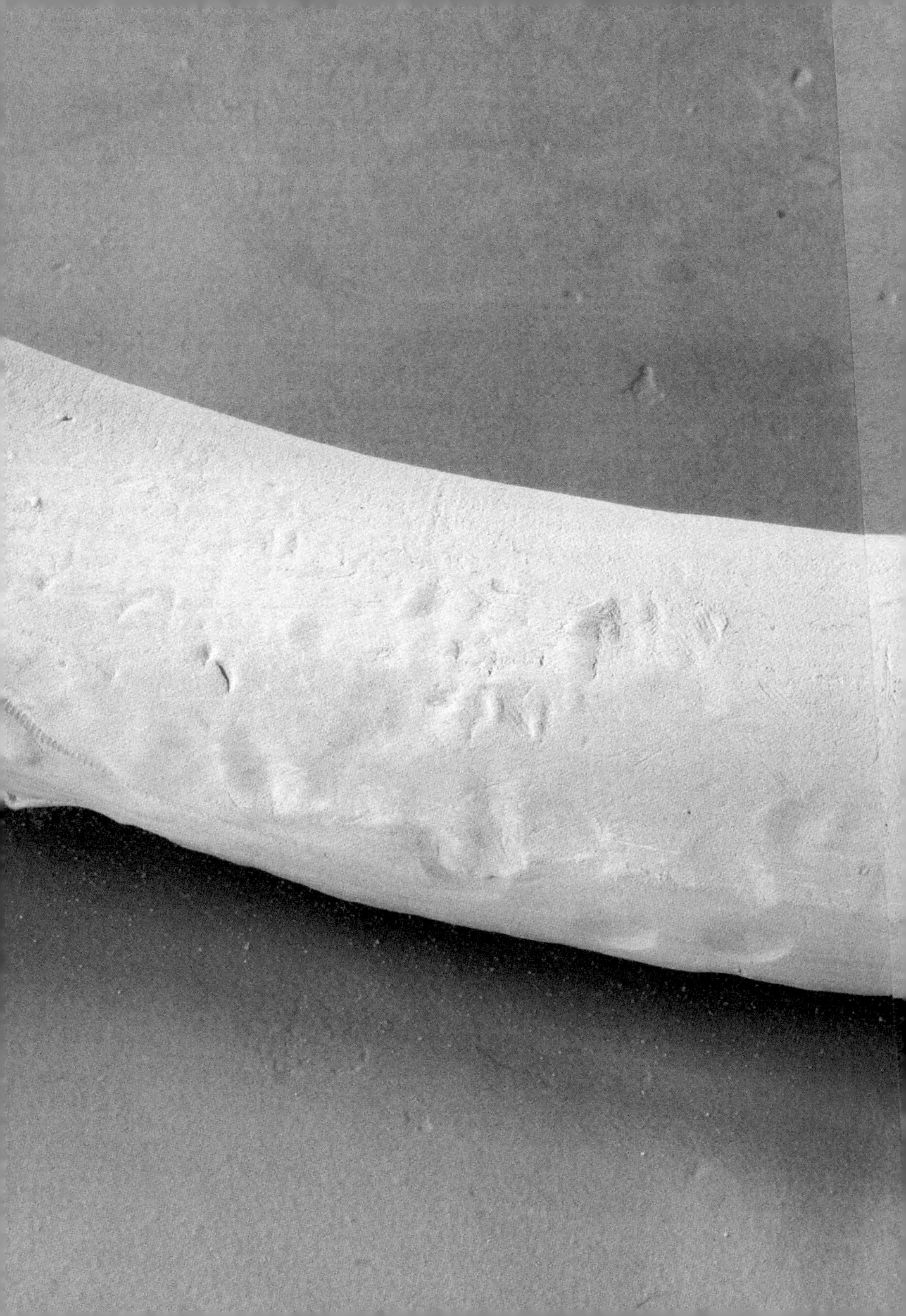

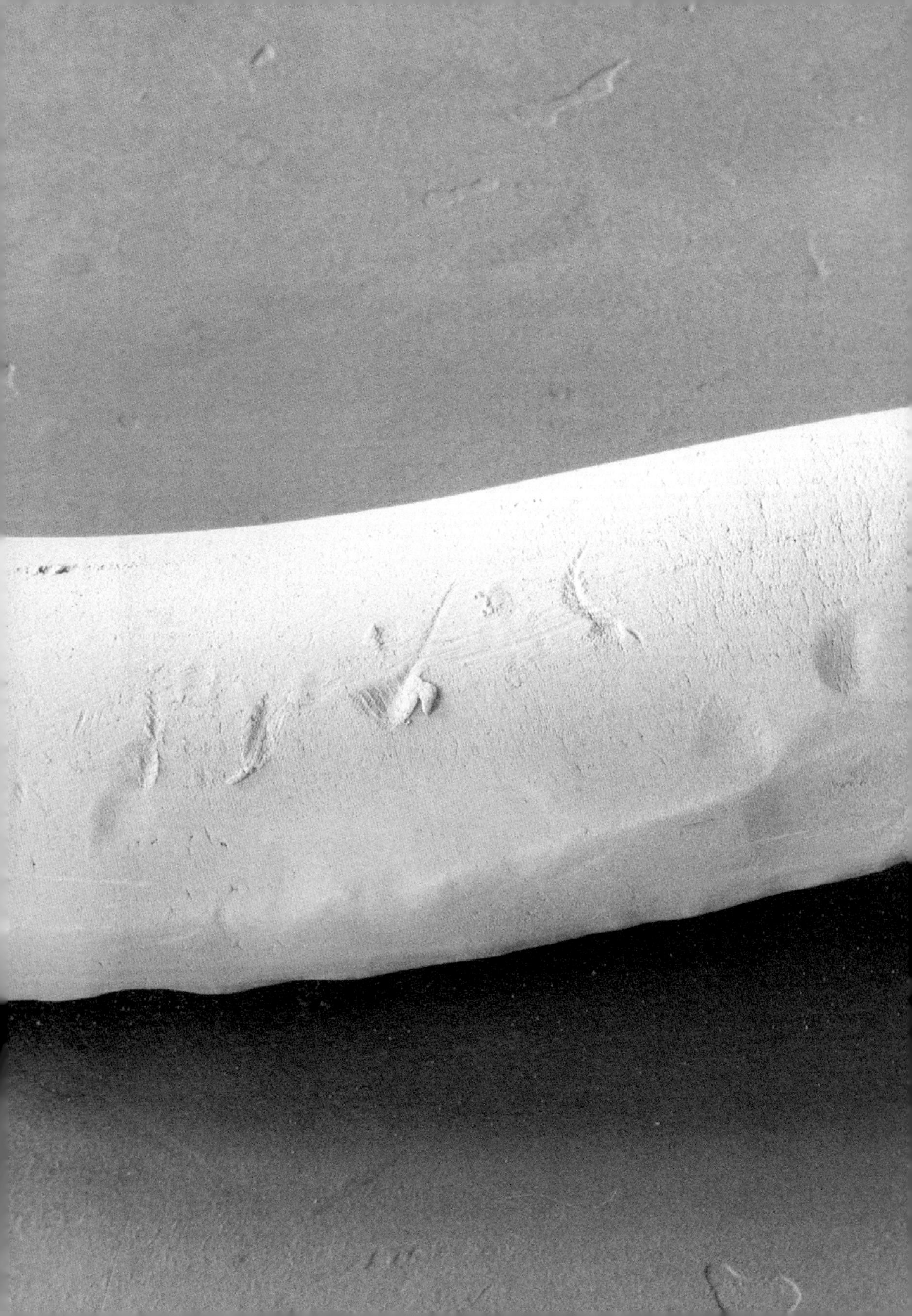

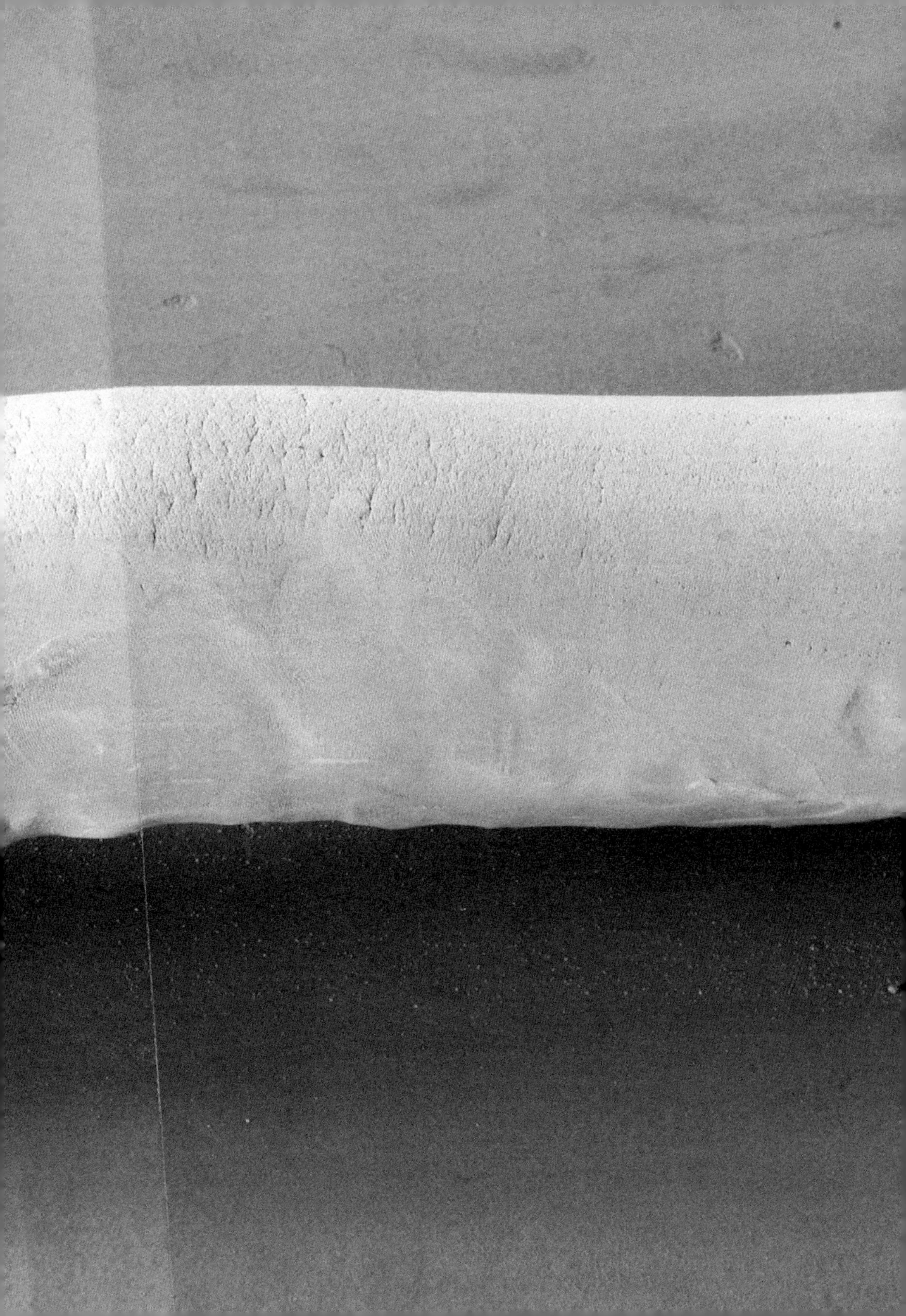

Light Switch, 2010
Bambus und aufgedampftes Aluminium auf Silikat-Glas

Die Transparenz dieses Objekts ändert sich, sobald
man es öffnet.

Light Switch, 2010
Bamboo and evaporated aluminum on silicate glass

The transparency of the object changes when
it is opened.

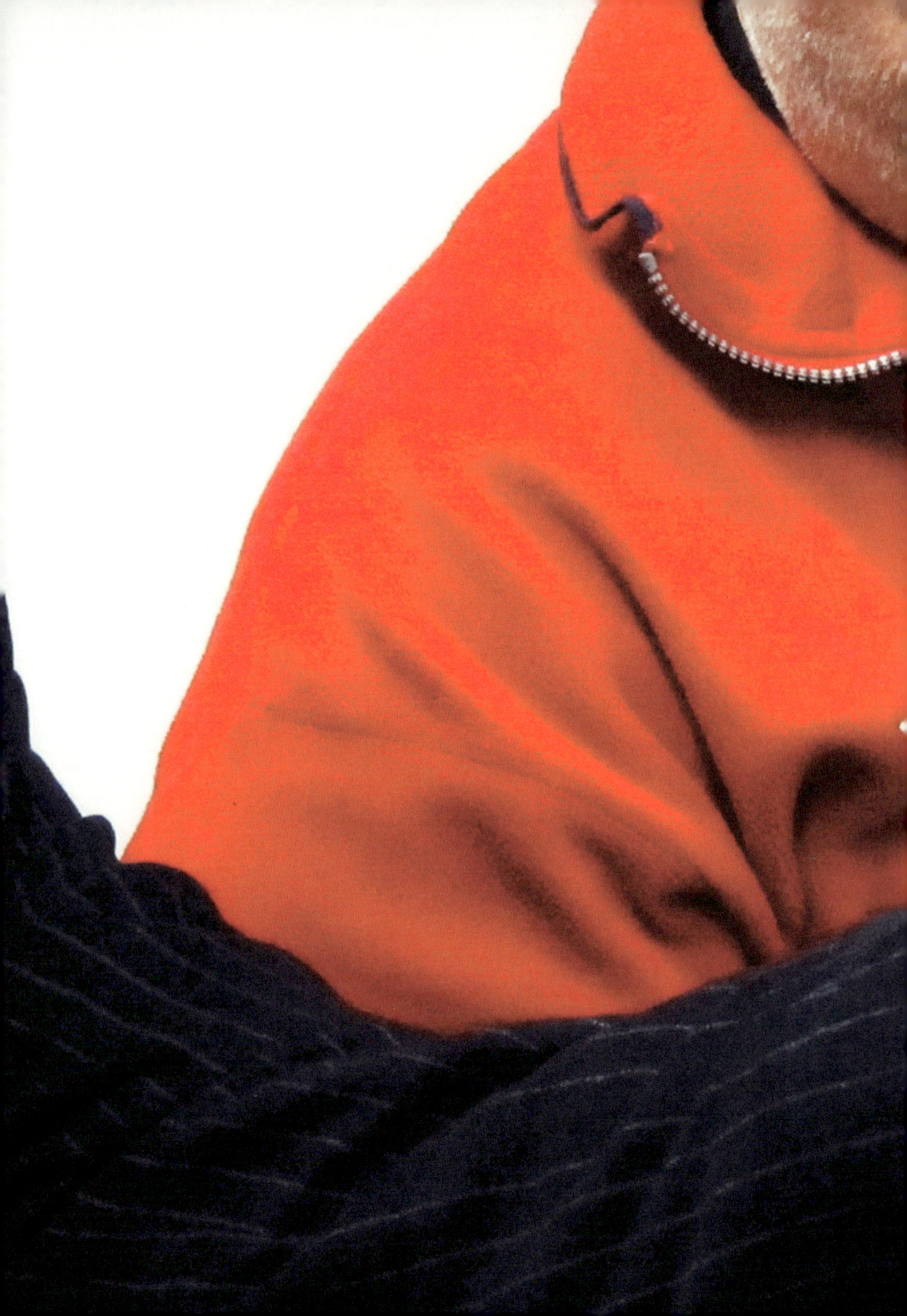

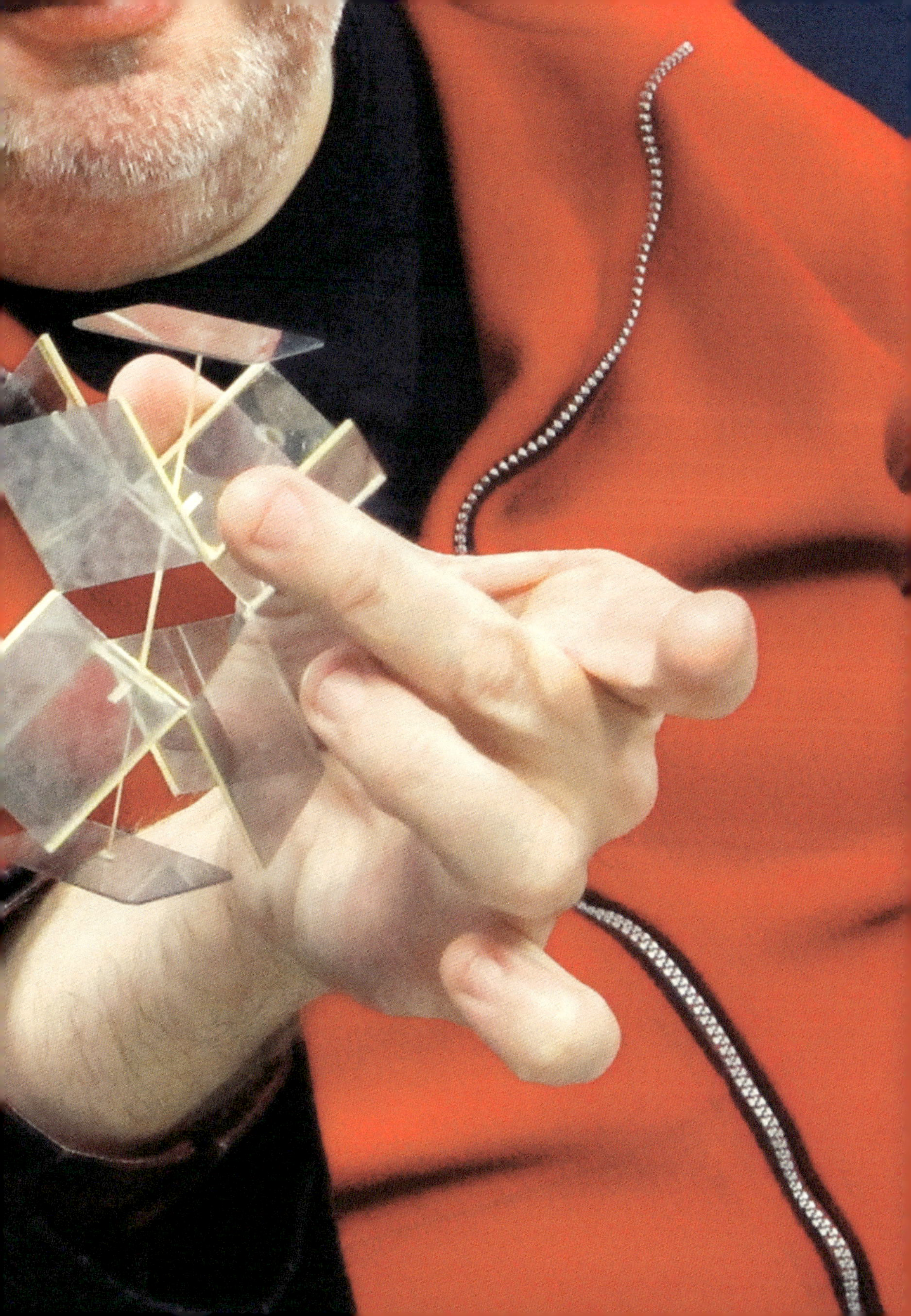

**7 Grams of Traces by the City of
Belo Horizonte, 2012**
Papier und Straßenstaub

Eine Papierrolle, die ich, in einem Ausstellungsraum
beginnend, durch die Straßen von Belo Horizonte
in Brasilien entrollte. Als die Papierbahn vollständig
ausgerollt war, habe ich sie wieder bis dahin, wo ich
angefangen hatte, eingerollt. Darin sammelten sich
alle Spuren, welche die Stadt auf dem Papier
hinterlassen hatte.

7 Grams of Traces by the City of
Belo Horizonte, 2012
Paper and street dust

A paper roll that I unrolled, starting from the exhibition
space through the streets of Belo Horizonte, Brazil.
After reaching the end of the paper, I rolled it back up
the way I came, collecting traces of the city in the
process.

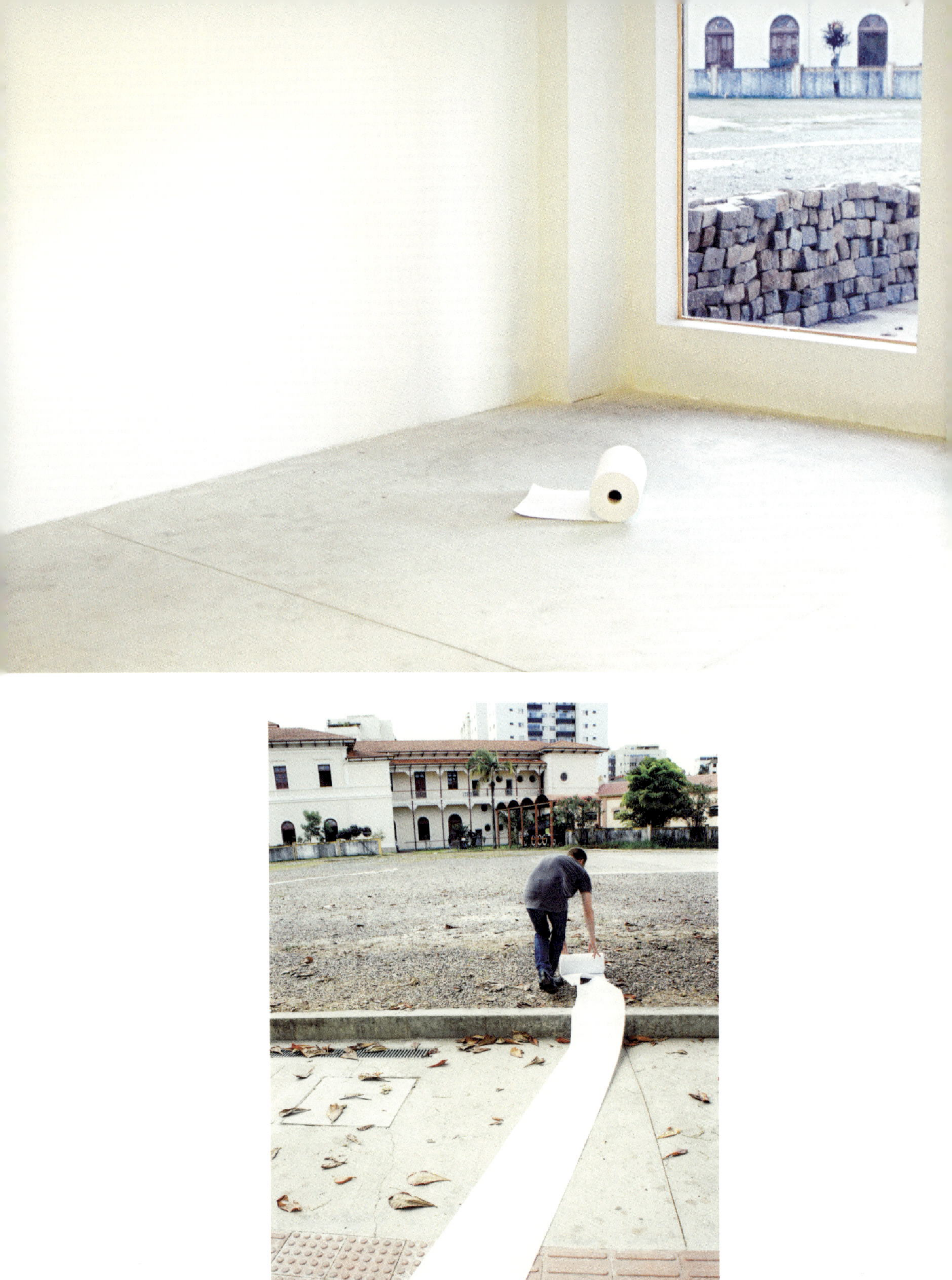

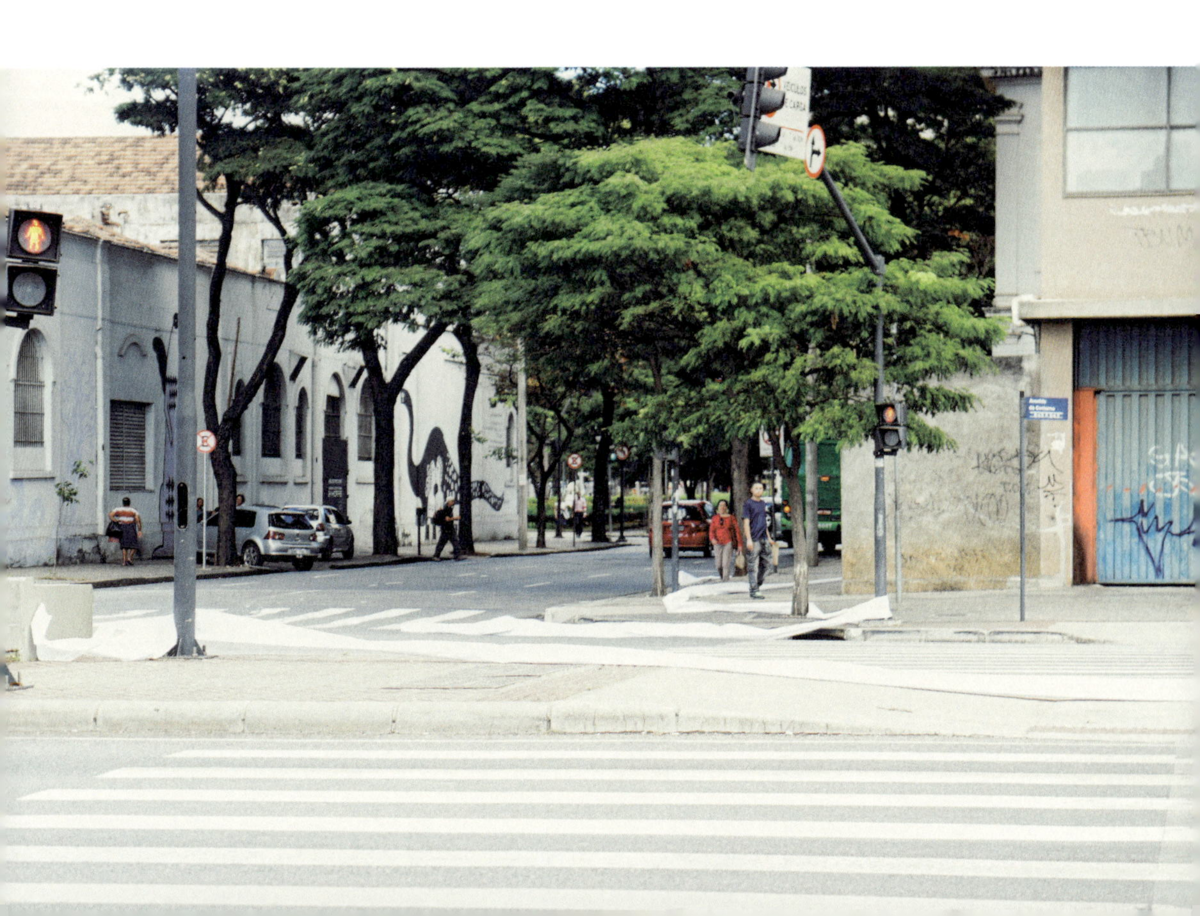

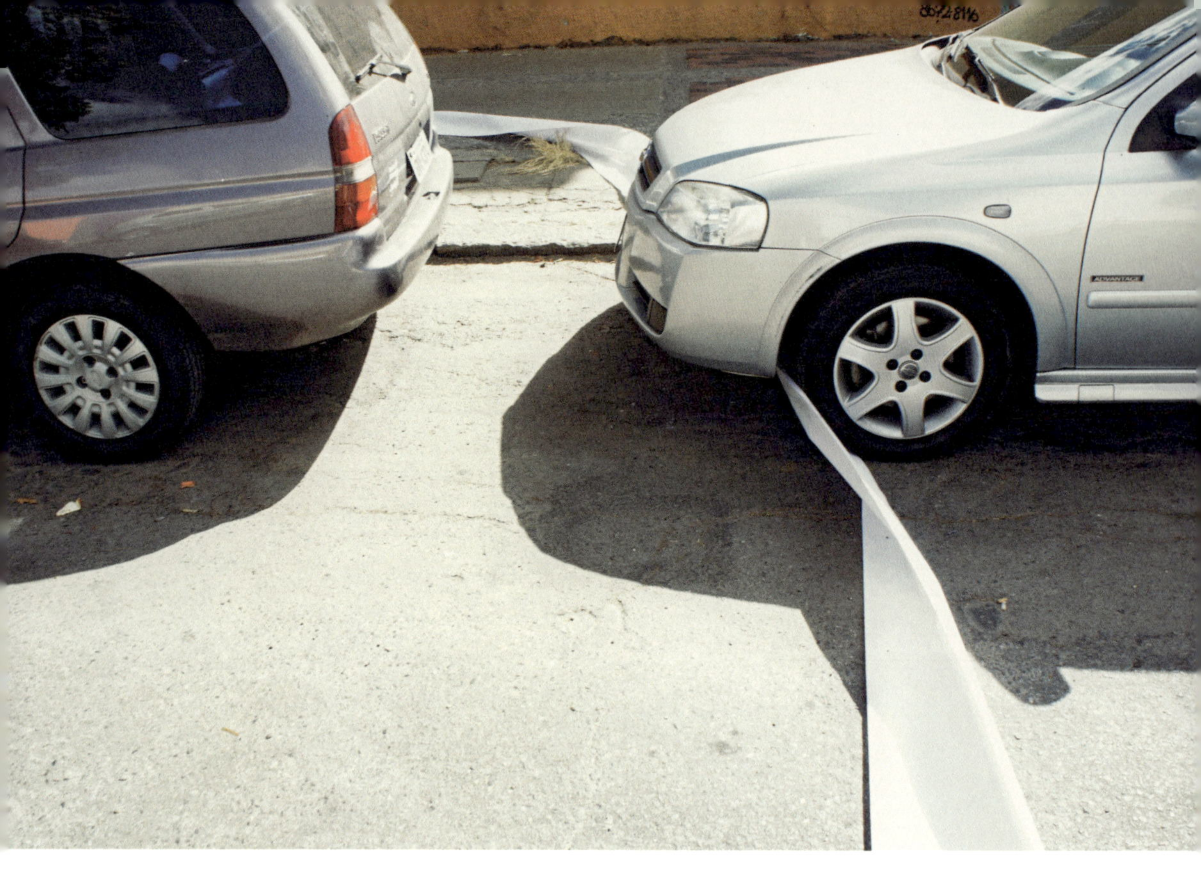

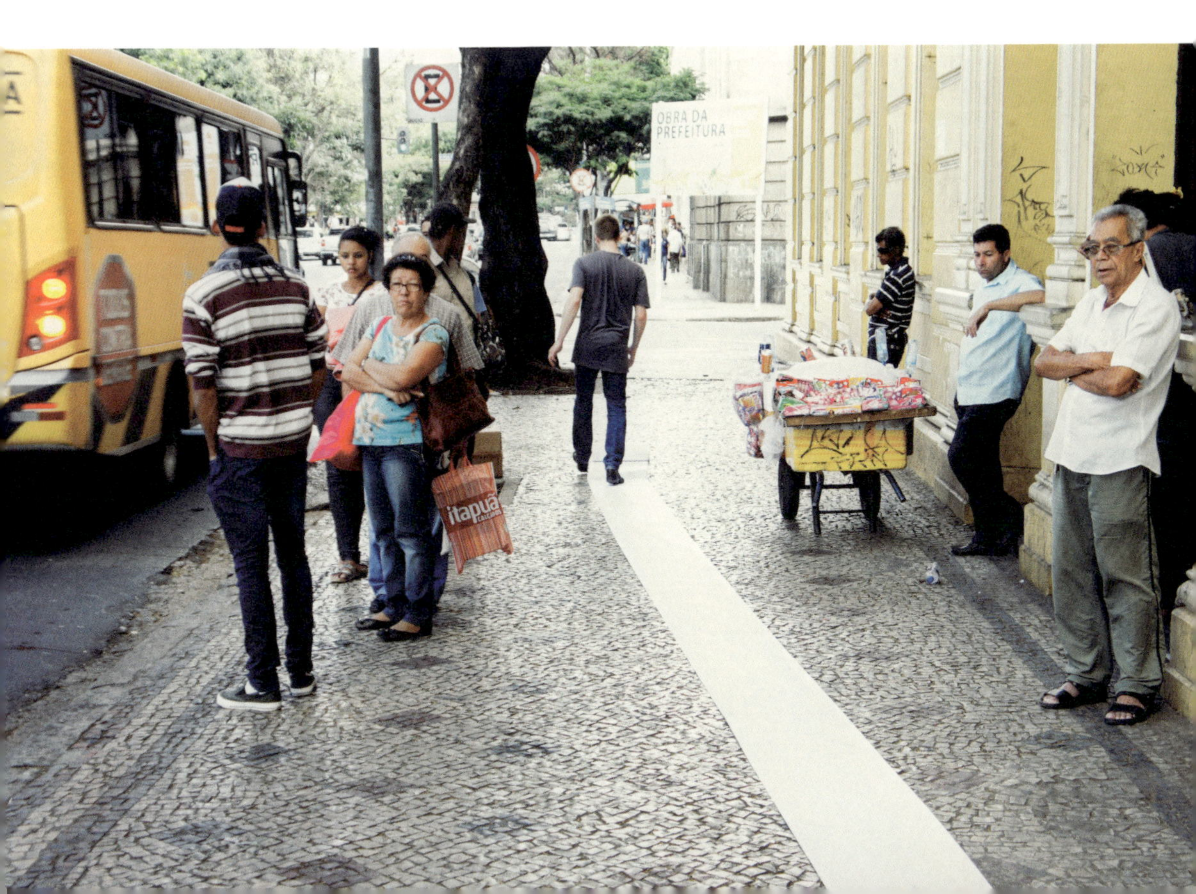

OBRA DA
PREFEITURA
itapuã

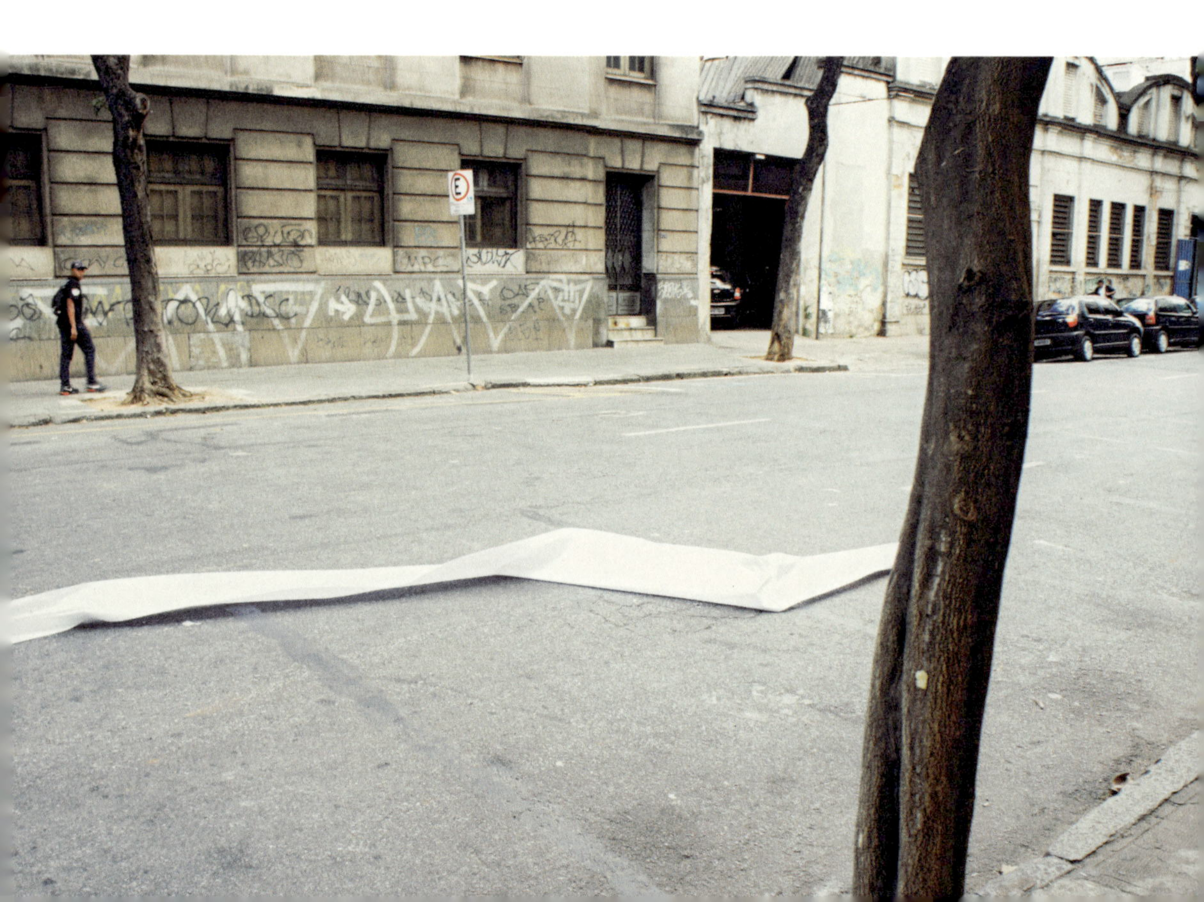

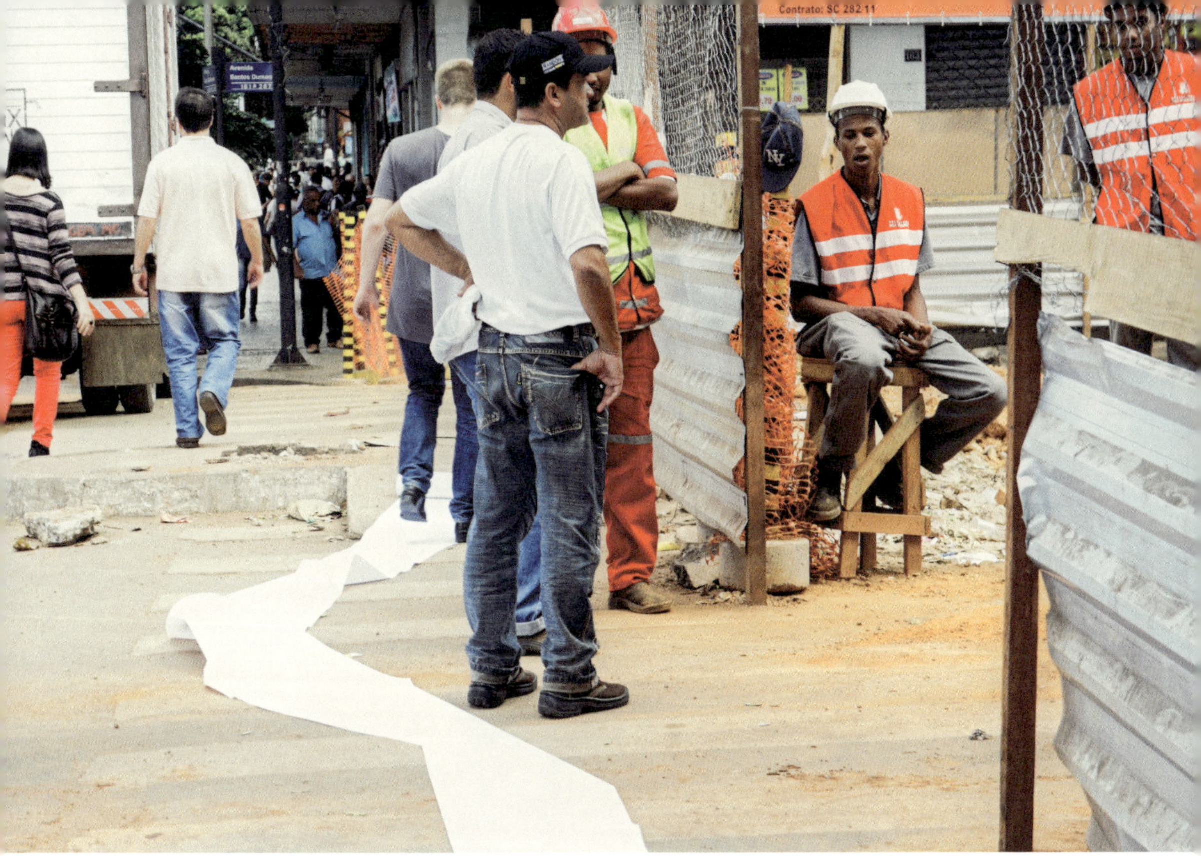

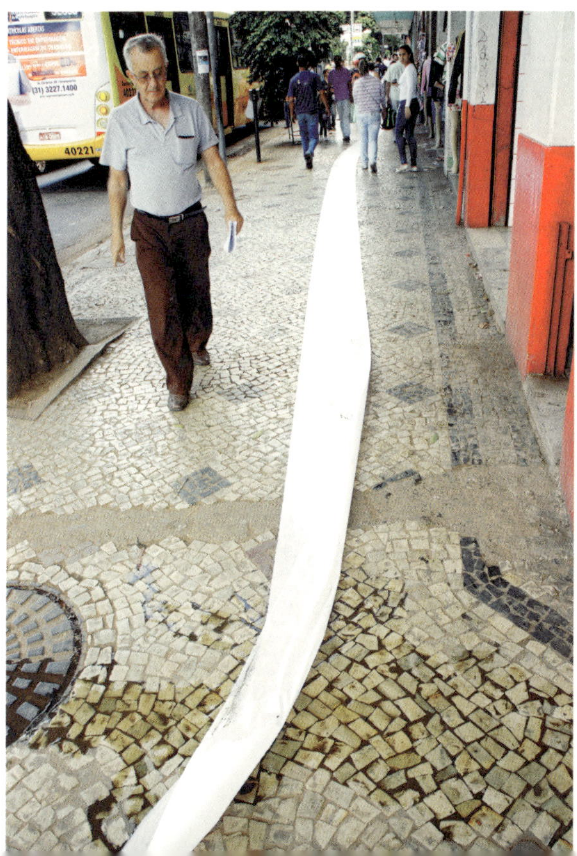

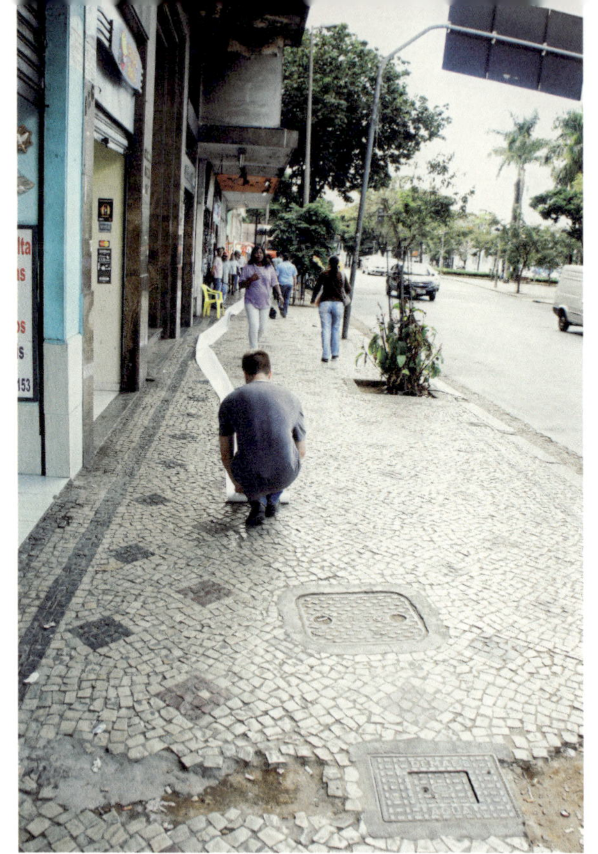

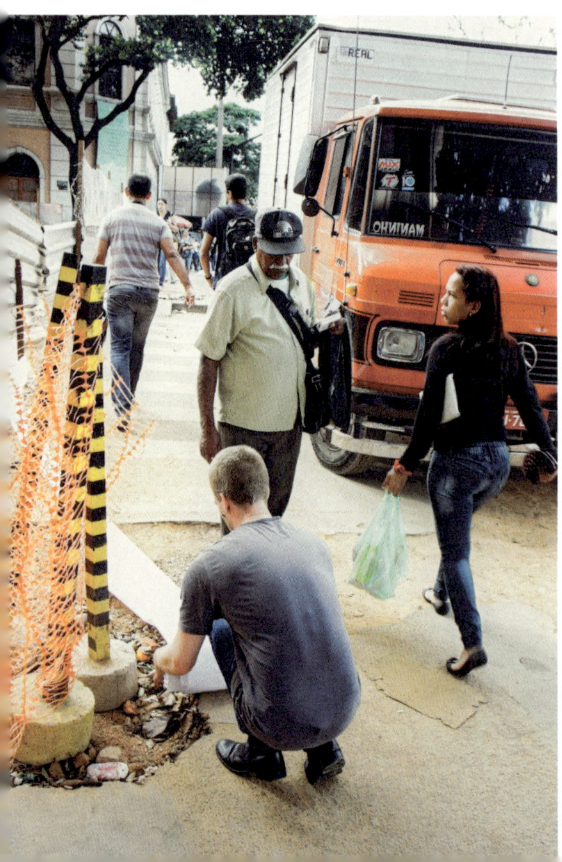

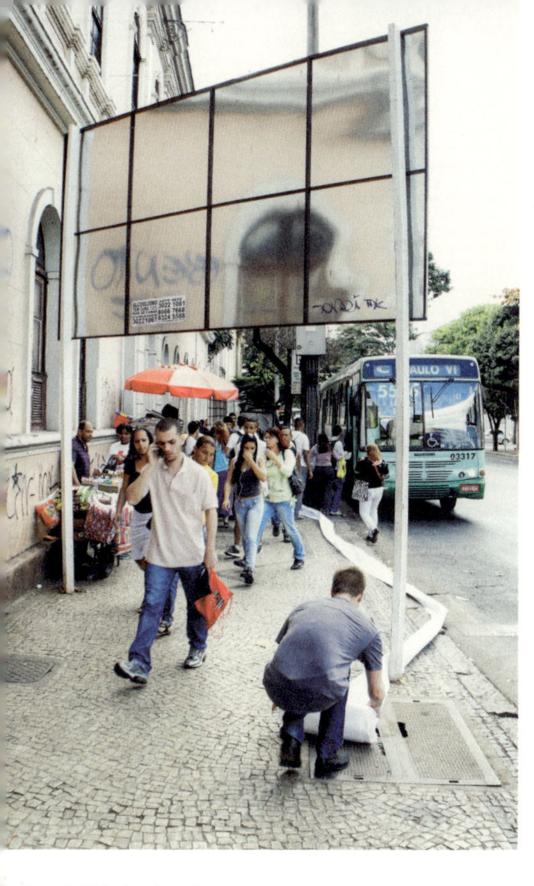

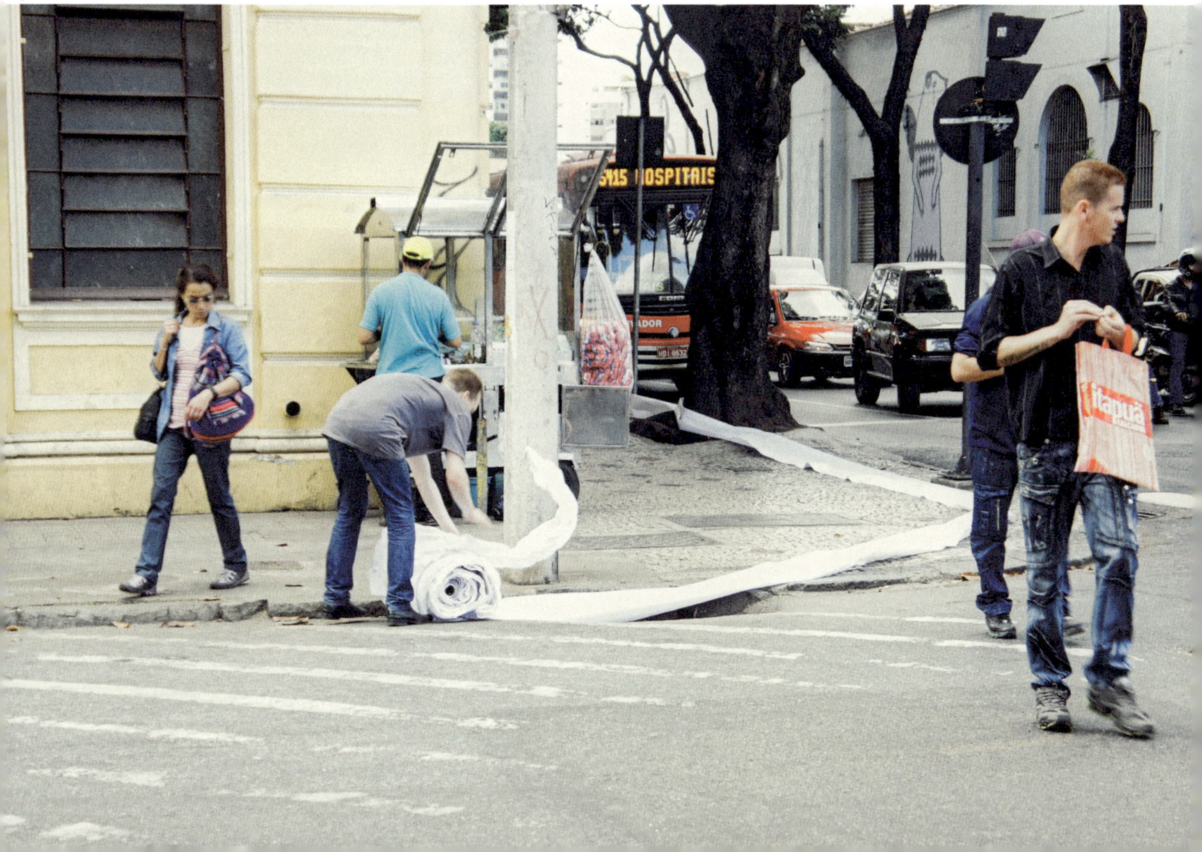

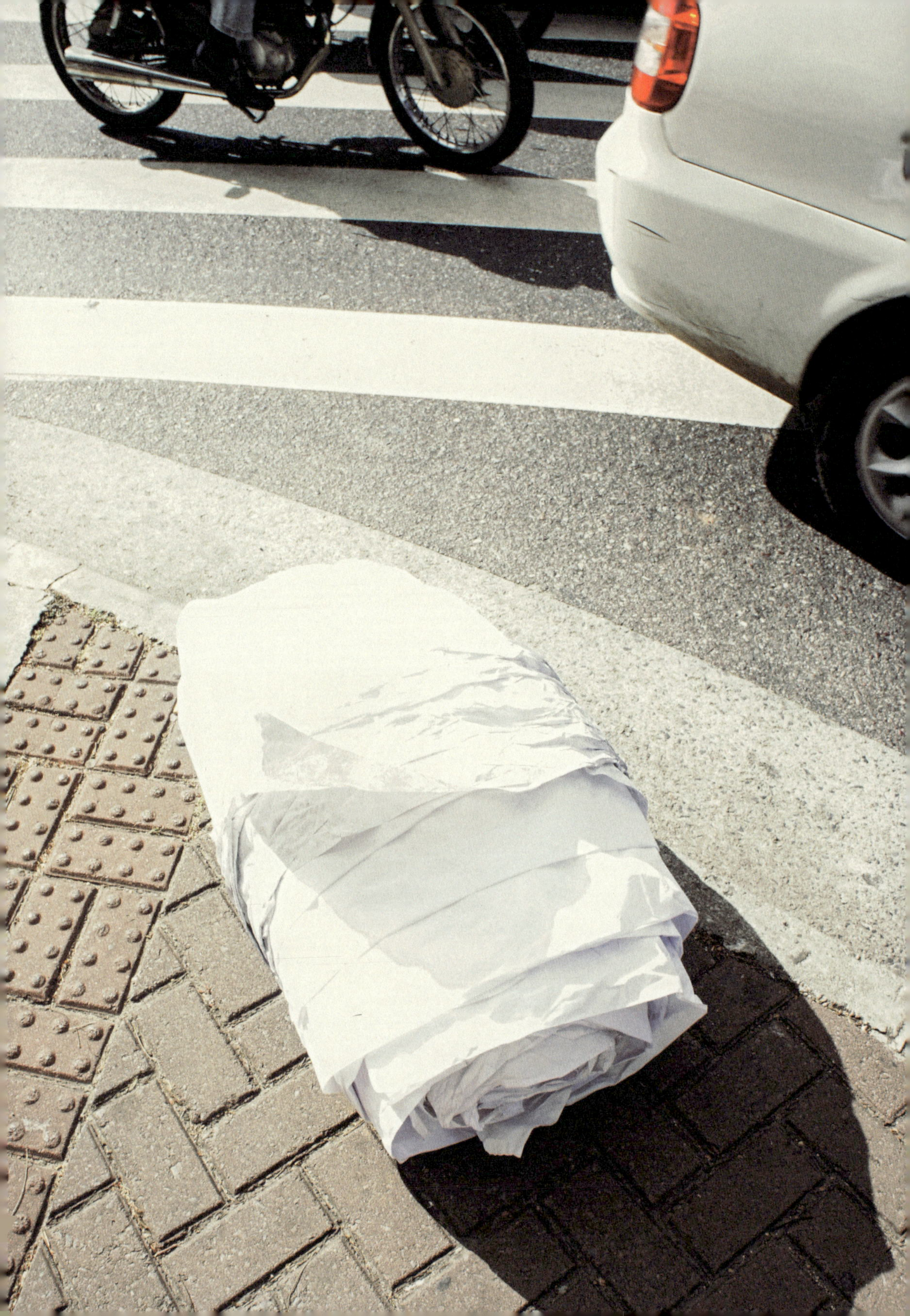

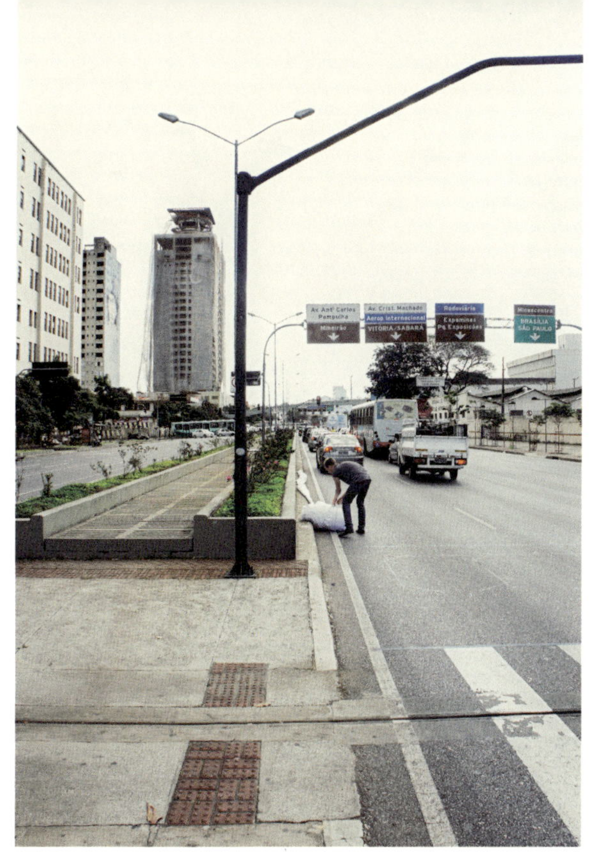

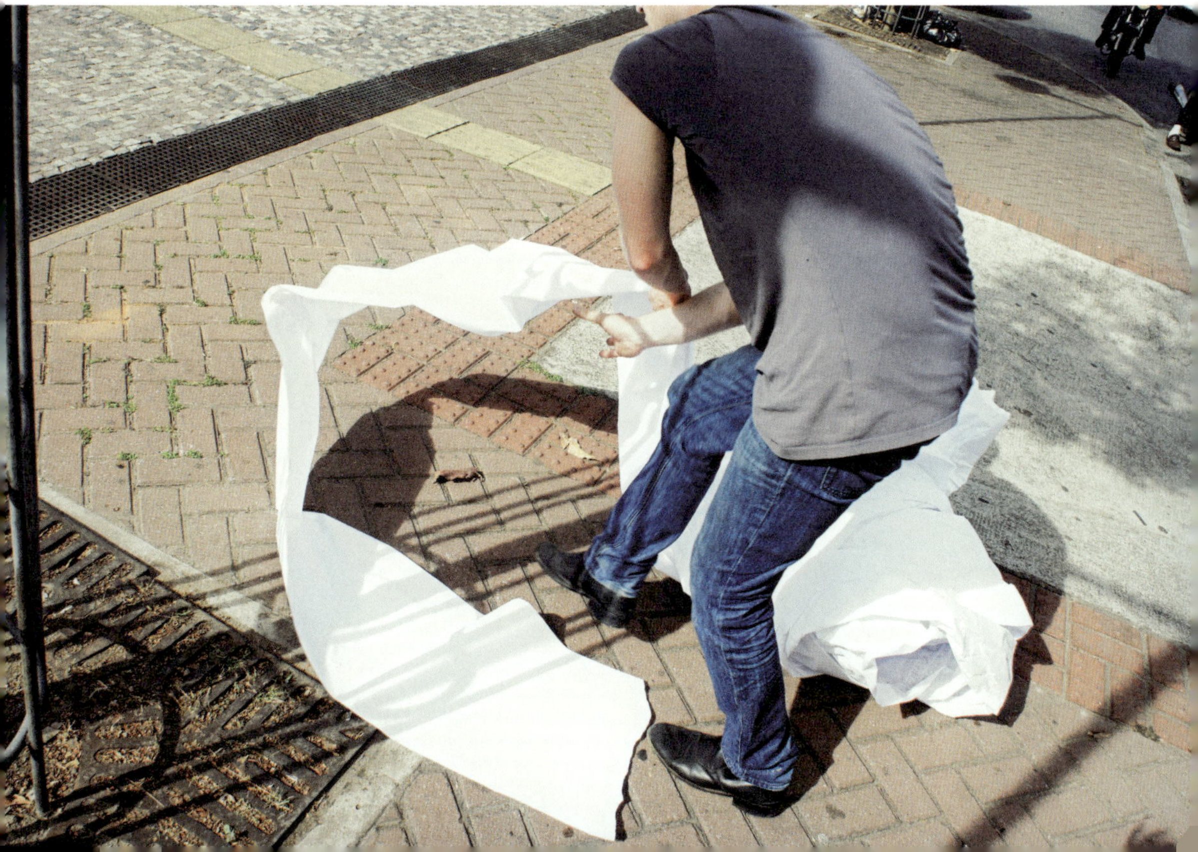

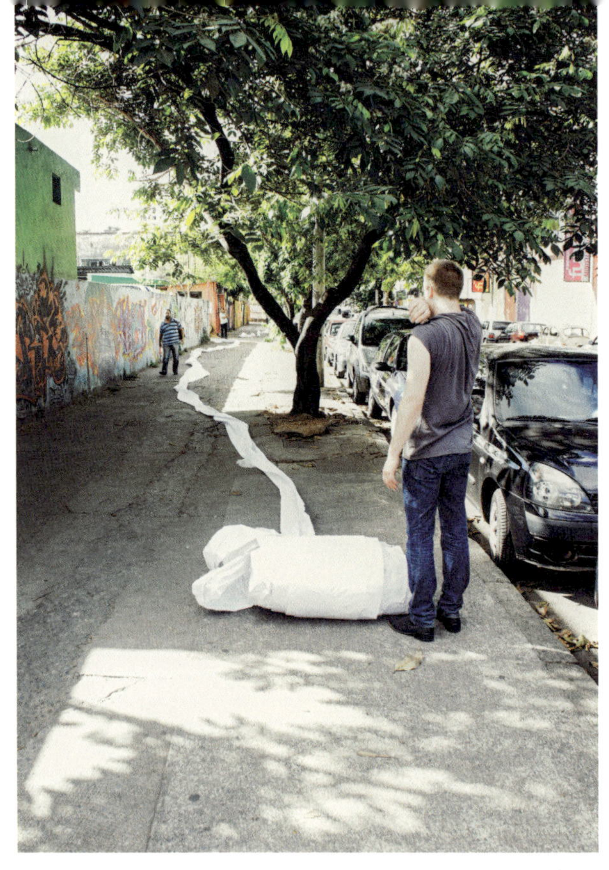

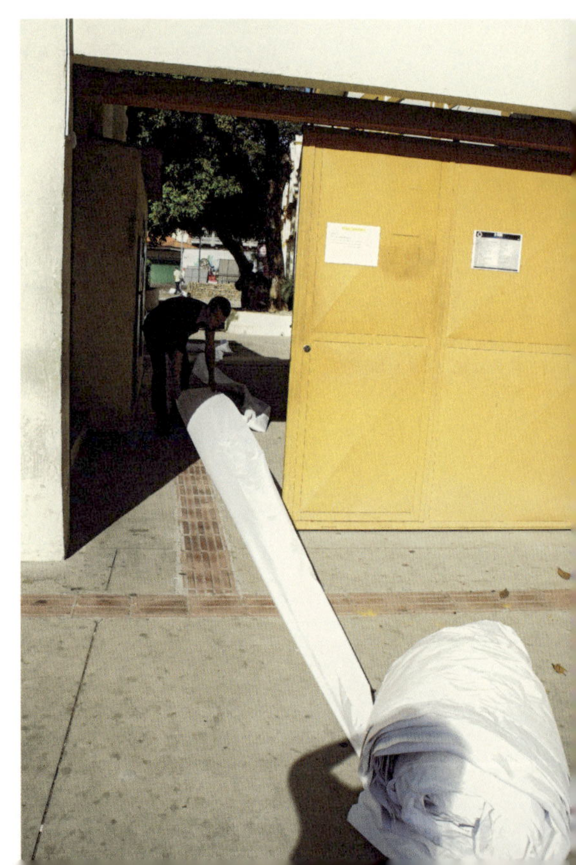

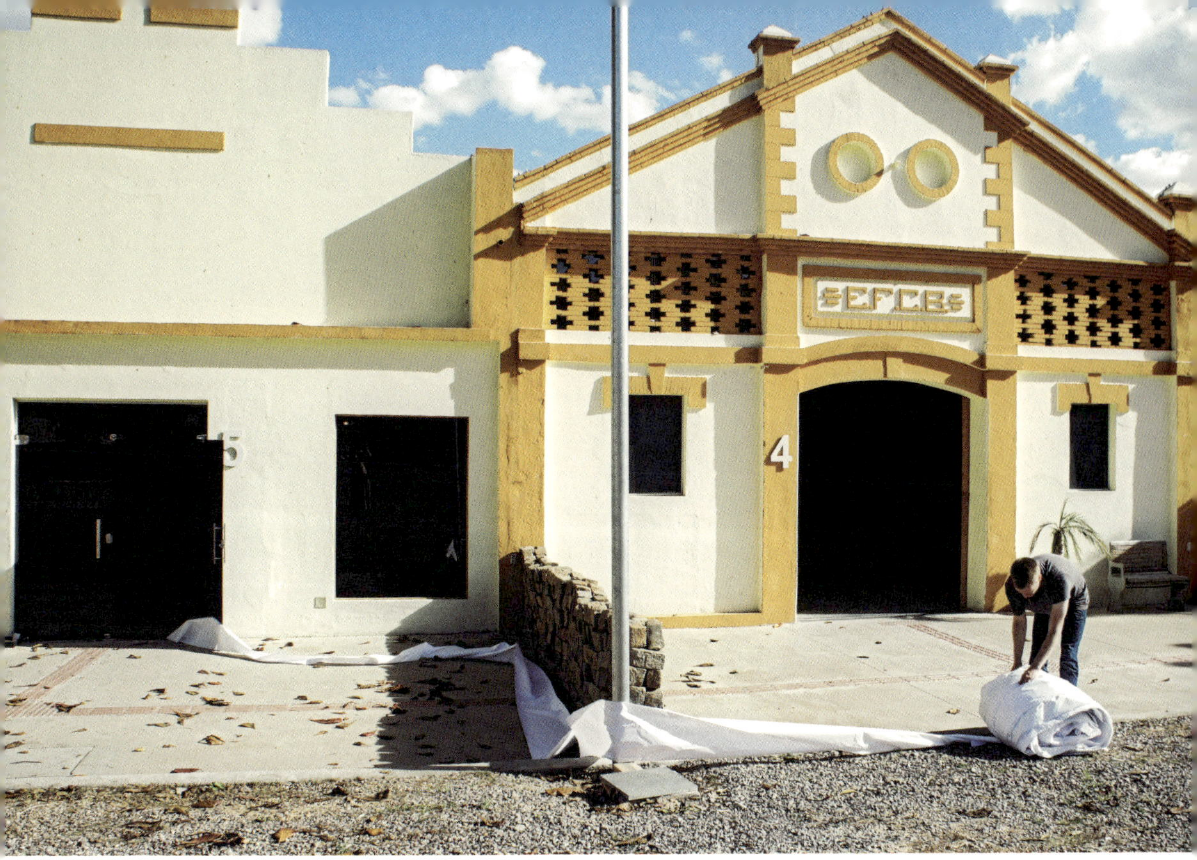

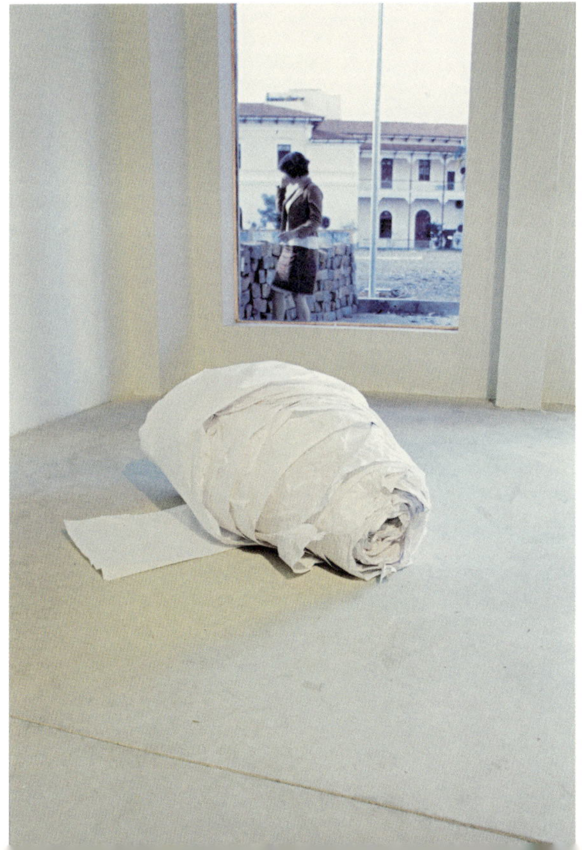

More than Happiness, 2012
Spiegel

Diese dauerhafte Installation wurde im Künstlerraum Billytown in Den Haag eingerichtet, in dem die Fenster durch zweiundfünfzig Spiegel ersetzt wurden.

More than Happiness, 2012
Mirror

This permanent installation, in which the windows have been replaced by fifty-two mirrors, was created for the artist-run space Billytown in the Hague.

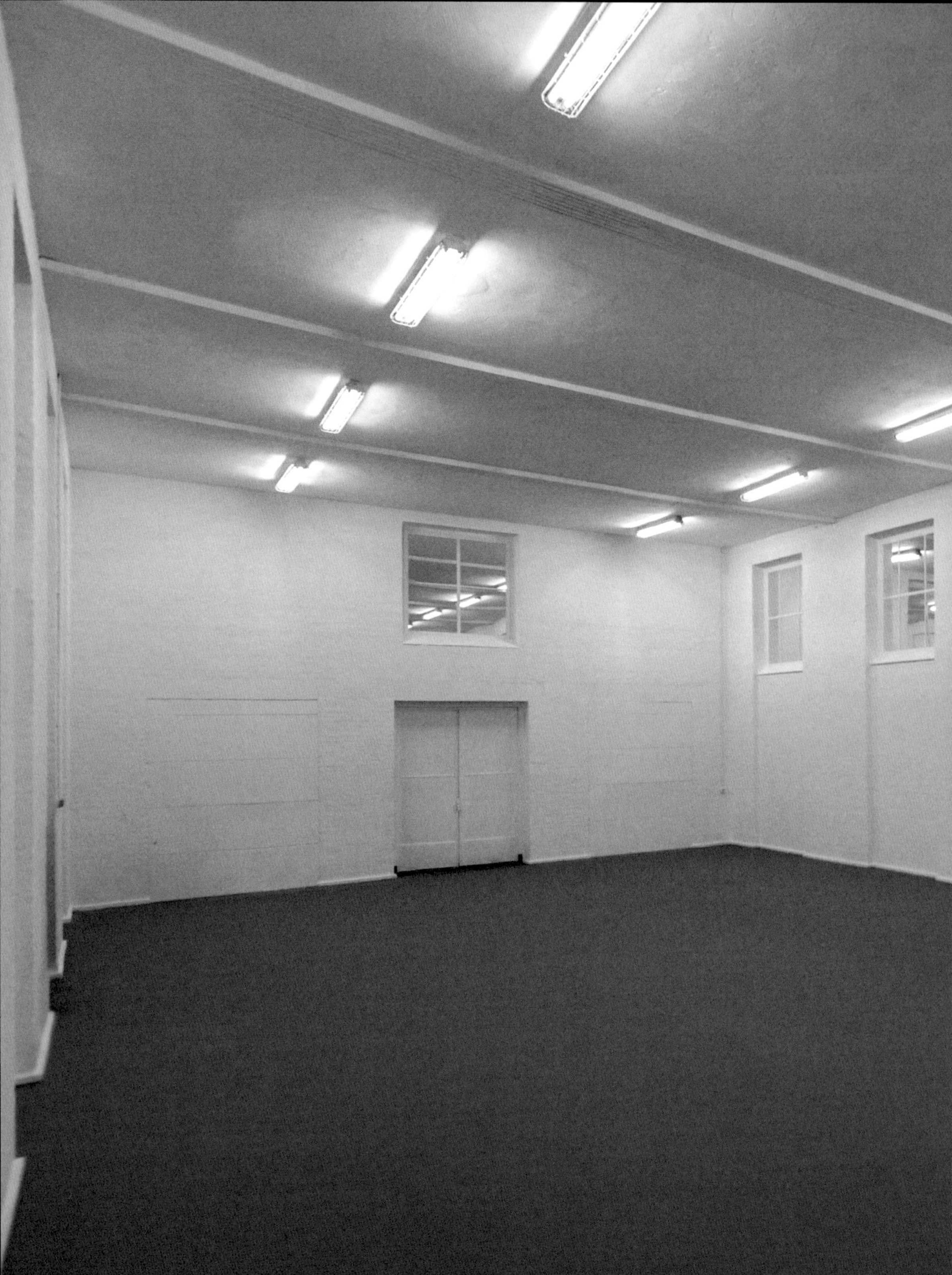

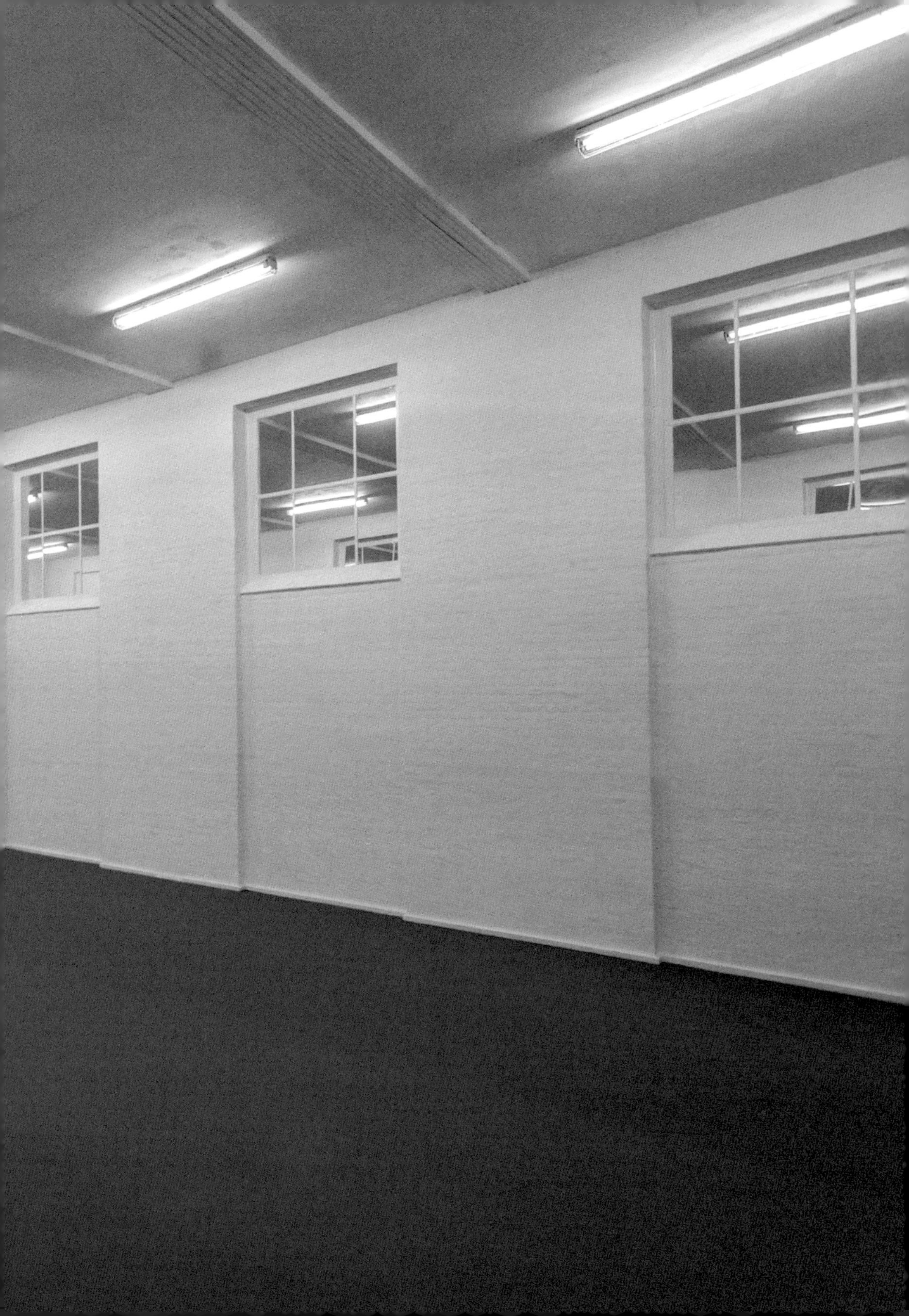

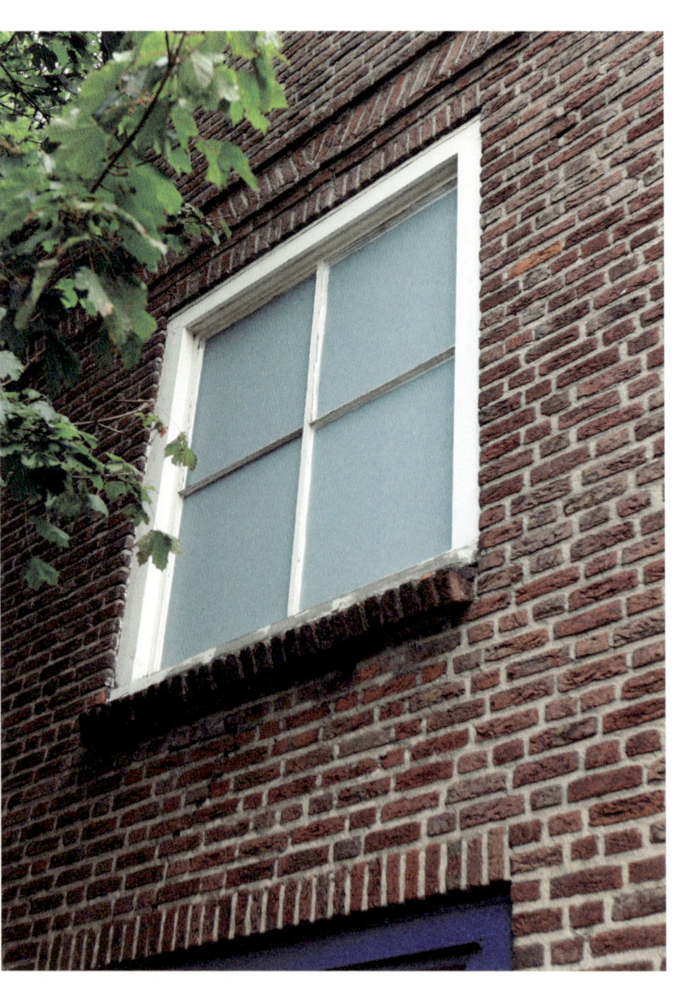

Du musst verstehn!
Aus Eins mach' Zehn,*
aus Null mach Zwei,
so bist du frei!   Silke Opitz

Mit seinen Arbeiten kehrt Maarten Sleeuwits nahezu
alle herkömmlichen Erwartungen um, die man
gegenüber derartigen Objekten im Kunstkontext
haben könnte. Weder handelt es sich um Skulpturen
einer neuen Minimal Art noch werden die weniger
großen Werke als Multiples produziert. Doch auch
original-einmalige Kleinplastiken, die sich und ihr
Material feiern würden, stellen diese Objekte nicht
wirklich dar, denn man soll sie nicht – wie einst der
Connaisseur – »gebildet« und still für sich allein,
sondern gern unvoreingenommen und mindestens
zu zweit in die Hände nehmen. Mehr noch, sie sind

See how it's done!
Make ten of one,*
From zero make two,
That's freedom for you!   Silke Opitz

Maarten Sleeuwits's works turn our usual
expectations for such art-world objects on their
heads. They are neither sculptures belonging to a
new kind of Minimal Art, nor are the smaller pieces
among them produced as multiples. The objects
also cannot really be regarded as unique statuettes
celebrating their originality and their materials.
For they are not meant to be contemplated quietly
and privately from a "cultivated" distance, as a
connoisseur might once have done; instead, we
are encouraged to pick them up and handle them
with an open mind and to share the experience

ausdrücklich zu benutzen, denn erst durch
Anwendung finden sie Vollendung. Dabei erfüllen
sie wiederum keine Funktion im strengen und vor
allem bekannten Sinne, sodass sie sich trotz ihrer
puristischen Gestalt auch schlecht dem Design
zuordnen lassen. Es ist alles viel einfacher.

Sleeuwits demonstriert Materialien und Formen
und macht diese für den Betrachter nachhaltig
erlebbar. Blei und Ton, Porzellan und Bambus sind
nur einige Rohstoffe und Mischsubstanzen, mit
denen sich der Künstler beschäftigt und die er
mittels seiner Objekte sinnlich vermittelt. Letztere
dienen als eine Art »slow gadgets« auch dazu,
den im Wesentlichen auf Aluminium-Silikat-Glas
ausgerichteten Tastsinn des Menschen im digitalen
Zeitalter zu sensibilisieren, wenn nicht zu reaktivieren.

with at least one other person. More than that,
these objects are expressly made to be used,
because it is only their use that makes them
complete. And yet they don't fulfill any function in
the narrower and, above all, familiar sense, so that
despite their purist form, they cannot be classified
as design objects. It is all much simpler than that.

Sleeuwits showcases the materials and forms
and turns them into a memorable experience for
the viewer. Lead and clay, porcelain and bamboo
are only a few of the raw materials and composite
substances with which the artist engages and
whose qualities he sensually conveys through his
objects. In our digital age rife with aluminosilicate
glass touchscreens, these objects act like "slow
gadgets" to heighten and even reactivate our sense

So kann man etwa einen massiven, mit Spezialkeramik
0,2 Millimeter dünn ummantelten Kubus aus
24 Karat Gold durch Fingerdruck wie einen
Zauberwürfel bewegen und dessen Form verändern.
Auch das Gewicht und die Oberflächenbeschaffenheit
der Materialien sind dabei zu spüren. Sleeuwits'
Arbeit Zero – mithilfe von Goldschmieden und
Keramiktechnikern aufwendig entwickelt – erfordert
Zeit und appelliert an die Feinmotorik der Rezipienten.
Das kleine Objekt verkörpert nicht nur seiner
Bezeichnung nach einen essenziellen Nullpunkt.
Es demonstriert Sinnentleerung durch Verdichtung
von Materie und führt somit bei seiner Anwendung
zu einer relativ ursprünglichen Wahrnehmung zurück.
Man weiß nicht genau, was einen erwartet. Oder
anders ausgedrückt: Nicht alles, was nicht glänzt,
ist nicht Gold.

of touch. Viewers get the chance, for example,
to alter the shape of a solid twenty-four-carat gold
cube clad in a 0.2-millimeter-thin skin of a special
ceramic—with just a squeeze, like magic. As they
do so, they get a feel for the weight and surface
properties of the materials. Sleeuwits's work
Zero—the product of an elaborate development
process in collaboration with goldsmiths and
ceramics engineers—takes time to comprehend
and appeals to the observer's fine motor skills.
It is not by name only that the tiny object embodies
a fundamental zero point. The way matter is
condensed within it also tangibly demonstrates the
erosion of meaning and thus leads us back, through
its use, to a relatively original state of perception.
You don't quite know what to expect. Or, to put it
another way: not all that does not glitter is not gold.

Um diese Ungewissheit des Rezipienten, mehr noch aber dessen daraus resultierende Neugier und Konzentration zu steigern, hat Sleeuwits die japanische Künstlerin Lei Saito gebeten, eine Ver- und Entpackungstechnik für Zero zu entwickeln. Nahezu rituell wird das Objekt vor den Augen des Betrachters erst (aus einem Seidentuch) enthüllt, um diesem dann präsentiert und in die Hand gegeben zu werden.

Schon den modernen Menschen hatte Vilém Flusser als in Folge von Überfrachtung – etwa durch Technik, Bilder und Begriffe – vereinsamt beschrieben. Das mag auch nach der Postmoderne noch so sein, und Flussers Gegenmittel, »Dinge so anzusehen, als sähe man sie das erste Mal«, wäre daher noch immer gefragt.[1] Zero ermöglicht diese Aneignungsmethode

In order to intrigue viewers even further, or, even more, to whet their curiosity and focus their concentration, Sleeuwits asked the Japanese artist Lei Saito to develop a wrapping and unwrapping method for Zero. The object is unveiled almost ritually before the beholder's eyes (while being removed from a silk cloth) and then presented to him and placed in his hand.

Decades ago, Vilém Flusser already described the loneliness of modern man as a consequence of mental overload—too much technology, too much imagery, too many concepts to deal with. Things have not changed much in our postmodern era, and so Flusser's antidote of "looking at things as if seeing them for the first time" is still just as beneficial as ever. In a certain sense,[1] Zero allows

in gewisser Weise. Statt den auch in der Kunst stetig wachsenden, hierarchischen Diskurs fortzusetzen, lässt Sleeuwits den Betrachter nicht durch Begriffe, sondern durch Begreifen begreifen. Mittels seiner Arbeiten eröffnet der Künstler Plattformen für unmittelbare Dialoge – zwischen Ding und Mensch sowie von Mensch zu Mensch.

Während **Zero** sich mit glatter, kühler Oberfläche als sanft und geschmeidig, seinem Gewicht nach eher als schwer über die Hand in das Gedächtnis des Anwenders einschreibt, behält es dabei seine zwar variable, aber grundlegende geometrische Form bei. Demgegenüber haben die Abdrücke von achtundzwanzig Händen die Arbeit **Recording No. 2** erst vollendet. Der 9,5 Meter lange, aus einfachem Ton bestehende Zylinder speichert physikalische Größen

for this kind of immediacy. Instead of carrying on the kind of hierarchical discourse that is on the rise in the art world, Sleeuwits helps viewers to grasp things not through dry concepts but through actually—well—grasping things. The artist opens up platforms for direct dialogue—between thing and person, as well as between two individuals.

While **Zero**, with its smooth, cool surfaces, inscribes itself via the hand into the user's memory as a soft and supple yet quite heavy thing, it nonetheless retains its variable but basic geometric form. By contrast, **Recording No. 2** is only complete once the imprints of twenty-eight hands have been incorporated into it. The 9.5-meter-long simple clay cylinder stores the physical quantities, such as force and motion, that must be summoned to budge a

wie Kraft und Bewegung, die aufgebracht werden
mussten, um ein Gewicht von 135 Kilogramm zu
bewältigen: Vierzehn Helfer haben die mittels eines
Tonschneiders vorgeformte, feuchte und schwere
Masse aus der Keramikwerkstatt der Amsterdamer
Rijksakademie van beeldende kunsten direkt in den
dortigen Ausstellungsraum getragen, wo sie
trocknete. Sleeuwits' Aktion, die das Objekt erst
hervorbrachte, ist diesem gleichsam eingedrückt.
An dessen Oberfläche zeichnen sich minimale
Spuren ab, die den Anteil der vierzehn partizipierenden
Träger dokumentieren und sie mit dem Künstler
gemeinsam als Urheber ausweisen.

Sleeuwits' Arbeit 7 Grams of Traces by the
City of Belo Horizonte enthält einen Ausschnitt
der brasilianischen Stadt. Das durchaus skulpturale

weight of 135 kilograms: fourteen helpers carried
the damp and heavy mass, pre-formed using a pug
mill, from the ceramics workshop at Amsterdam's
Rijksakademie van beeldende kunsten and directly
into the exhibition space, where it was then left
to dry. Sleeuwits's performance, which produced the
object in the first place, is thus, so to speak, inscribed
upon it. Minimal traces can be seen across its
surface that document the part played by the
fourteen participating carriers and mark them as
the artist's coauthors.

Sleeuwits's 7 Grams of Traces by the City
of Belo Horizonte contains an extract of the
Brazilian city. The sculptural object consists
of a long roll of white paper that the artist started
to unroll from inside a gallery in Belo Horizonte,

Objekt besteht aus einer langen Bahn weißen Papiers, die der Künstler von einem Galerieraum in Belo Horizonte beginnend über Fußwege und Straßen hinweg aus- und wieder eingerollt hatte. Zwischen den kurvigen Lagen der am Ende mathematischen Spiralform ist 7 Gramm Straßenstaub und somit der Ort der Entstehung wie der Präsentation des Werks gespeichert. Auch Kunst- und urbaner Raum finden wie zwei Komponenten in dieser Arbeit zusammen.

Sleeuwits unterläuft mittels seiner teilweise auf Aktionen basierenden, skulpturalen Objekte nicht nur die Hierarchien des Diskurses und der Urheber-schaft, sondern auch die des Materials. Während in der klassischen Bildhauerei dem Vorkommen und Marktwert entsprechend streng zwischen echt und endgültig (Marmor, Bronze) oder unecht und

continuing on through pedestrian zones and streets and then rolling it back up again to return to the gallery. Between the curved layers in their final mathematical spiral form, seven grams of street dus are stored, and hence traces of the work's place of origin as well as its original presentation. The art space and the urban space are conjoined as two integral components of the work.

With his partially action-based sculptural objects, Sleeuwits subverts the hierarchies not only of the discourse and of authorship, but also that of the material. Whereas in classical sculpture a strict distinction was made in terms of rarity and market value between genuine and final works (marble, bronze) and copies or provisional studies (clay, plaster), for Sleeuwits all materials are of equal

vorläufig (Ton, Gips) unterschieden wurde, nivelliert
Sleeuwits diese Wertigkeit und betrachtet Materialien
als gleichberechtigte Elemente. Statt diese mittels
virtuos beherrschter Techniken veredeln zu wollen,
schätzt er sie vielmehr an sich wie auch ihres
inhärenten Potenzials wegen. Diesem Ansatz entspricht
in gewissem Sinne auch seine Gleichsetzung von
Werk und Werkzeug. Beide bedingen sich nicht nur
im Arbeitsprozess, sondern gehen manchmal auch
auseinander hervor, lösen einander ab: Um sein
mobiles wie taktiles Objekt Moving Bone China
zu verwirklichen, hatte Sleeuwits zunächst für die
Bearbeitung der Porzellanrohmasse eine metallene
Schneideschablone gefertigt. Gespiegelt ergab diese
dann den Prototyp für die spätere Arbeit Plumbum,
welche die leichte Verformbarkeit des Schwermetalls
vorführt und darin auch den Bewegungsmechanismus

value. Instead of attempting to refine them through
masterful techniques, he appreciates them for what
they are and for their own inherent potential. In a
sense, this approach is tantamount to equating work
with tool. The two are not only interdependent in
the work process; one sometimes gives rise to,
or replaces, the other. For example, to develop his
at once mobile and tactile object Moving Bone
China, Sleeuwits first made a cutting template out
of lead for working with the raw porcelain mass.
Mirrored, this cutting template then served as
prototype for the later work Plumbum, which
demonstrates the ductility of the heavy metal
and hence also comments on the movement that
produced the earlier rigid porcelain object.

des vorausgegangenen, an sich starren Porzellan-
objektes kommentiert.

Diese dialogischen Beziehungen zwischen Werk und
Werkzeug, Werk und Schöpfer oder Werk und
Betrachter beziehungsweise Anwender beschränken
sich ihrem Ort nach nicht auf die Werkstatt, das
Atelier oder die Ausstellung. Sleeuwits' Objekte
funktionieren auch darüber hinaus als Kommunikations-
mittel und sind besonders als Satellite(s) to Send
Away überall einsetzbar. Das fragile und ultraleichte
Werk aus Bambus in Form einer beweglichen,
doppelten Zickzacklinie ist einmal mehr zu nichts,
das man kennen würde, zu gebrauchen. Gerade
deshalb und weil es eigentlich auch unbeschreiblich
ist, sollte man es sich zuschicken lassen.

These dialogue-based relationships between work
and tool, work and creator, or work and viewer/user
are not limited to the workshop, studio, or exhibition
space where the objects are located. Sleeuwits's
objects instead go beyond their setting to function
as a means of communication, designed to be used
anywhere, as is Satellite(s) to Send Away. This
fragile and ultra-lightweight bamboo piece with the
form of a flexible, double zigzag line is once again
not useful for anything you could think of. But for
that very reason, and because it is so impossible
to describe, that you should really have it sent to you

* Die ersten zwei Zeilen
des Hexeneinmaleins aus:
Johann Wolfgang von
Goethe, Faust.
Eine Tragödie,
Tübingen 1808, S. 161.

[1] »Dinge so anzusehen,
als sähe man sie das erste
Mal, ist eine Methode, an
ihnen bisher unbeachtete
Aspekte zu entdecken.
Es ist eine gewaltige
und fruchtbare Methode,
aber sie erfordert strenge
Disziplin und kann
daher leicht misslingen«,
aus: Vilém Flusser,
Dinge und Undinge.
Phänomenologische
Skizzen, München 1993,
S. 53.

* The first two lines of the
witches' magic formula
(Hexeneinmaleins),
from Johann Wolfgang
von Goethe, Faust:
Eine Tragödie
(Tübingen, 1808), p. 161.
Translation from
Faust I & II, in
Goethe's Collected
Works, vol. 2, ed. and
trans. Stuart Atkins
(Boston, 1984), p. 65.

[1] "Looking at things
as if seeing them for the
first time is a method
for discovering aspects
that previously went
unnoticed. It is a powerful
and fertile method, but
it requires strict discipline
and can therefore easily
fail." in Vilém Flusser,
Dinge und Undinge:
Phänomenologische
Skizzen (Munich, 1993),
p. 53.

Maarten Sleeuwits wurde 1978 im niederländischen
Enschede geboren und studierte von 2000 bis 2005
an der Gerrit Rietveld Academie in Amsterdam.
Von 2010 bis 2011 nahm er am Künstlerprogramm
der Rijksakademie van beeldende kunsten Amsterdam
teil. Seine Arbeiten wurden europaweit in mehreren
Gruppenausstellungen gezeigt. Zudem ist er
Mitbegründer des Künstlerraums Kazachenko's
Apartment in Oslo. **Objects and Recordings** in der
Kunsthalle Erfurt stellt seine erste Einzelausstellung dar.

Maarten Sleeuwits was born in 1978 in Enschede,
the Netherlands, and studied at the Gerrit Rietveld
Academie in Amsterdam from 2000 until 2005.
He was artist-in-residence at the Rijksakademie van
beeldende kunsten, Amsterdam, from 2010 to 2011.
His work has been shown in several group exhibitions
across Europe, and he is one of the initiators of the
artist-run space Kazachenko's Apartment in Oslo.
Objects and Recordings showing at Kunsthalle
Erfurt marks Sleeuwits's first solo exhibition.

Ohne die Hilfe und Unterstützung folgender
Personen wäre dieses Buch nicht möglich gewesen:
Marleen Chang-Sleeuwits, Rogier und Hugo Chang,
Maarten Daudeij, Jasper Engel, Isabel Franke,
Henk Drosterij und Karen Knispel, Philipp Kremer,
Teun Oud, Nicholas Riis,Marieke Schoonderbeek,
Hans und Elise Sleeuwits sowie Ka Yuk und Aldwin
Tong Sleeuwits.

This book would not have been possible without
the help and support of the following people:
Marleen Chang-Sleeuwits, Rogier and Hugo Chang,
Maarten Daudeij, Jasper Engel, Isabel Franke,
Henk Drosterij and Karen Knispel, Philipp Kremer,
Teun Oud, Nicholas Riis, Marieke Schoonderbeek,
Hans and Elise Sleeuwits as well as Ka Yuk and
Aldwin Tong Sleeuwits.

Bildnachweis|Photo credits:
Sofern nicht anders angegeben, alle Bilder|Unless
otherwise stated all pictures Maarten Sleeuwits; Jasper
Engel: Chocolate; Rumiko Hagiwara: 7 Grams
of Traces by the City of Belo Horizonte; Hans
Sleeuwits: Moving Bone China.

Diese Publikation erscheint anlässlich der Ausstellung| This book is published in conjunction with the exhibition

Maarten Sleeuwits. Objects and Recordings

Kunsthalle Erfurt im Haus zum Roten Ochsen 9. Mai – 29. Juni 2014 May 9–June 29, 2014

Kunstmuseen der Stadt Erfurt Kunsthalle Erfurt im Haus zum Roten Ochsen Fischmarkt 7 99084 Erfurt Tel. +49 361 6555660 Fax +49 361 6555669 www.kunsthalle-erfurt.de

Ausstellung|Exhibition Kuratorin|Curator: Silke Opitz

Aufbau|Installation: Angelika Deege, Ramona Wild, Bernhard Werlich

Presse|Press: Rita Otto

Konservatorische Betreuung| Conservation assistance: Zentrale Restaurierungs- werkstätten der Museen der Stadt Erfurt|The central restoration workshops of the Museen der Stadt Erfurt

Registrar|Registrar: Marion Aschenbach

Sekretariat|Administration: Stefanie Mansfeld

Publikation|Publication Herausgeber|Editor: Silke Opitz und|and Landeshauptstadt Erfurt

Redaktion|Editing: Silke Opitz

Lektorat|Copyediting: Sandra-Jo Huber, Charlotte Neugebauer, Hatje Cantz

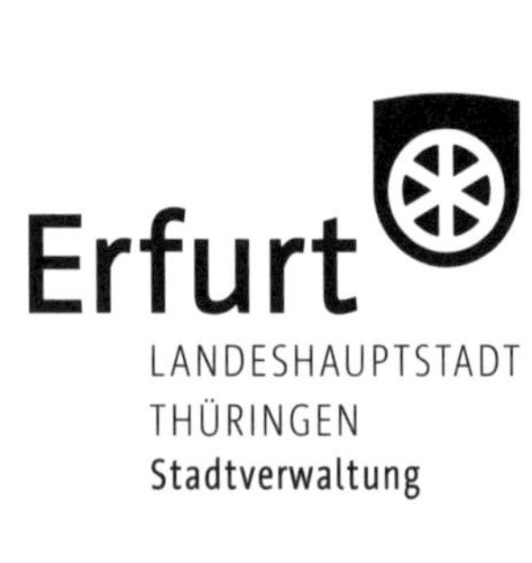

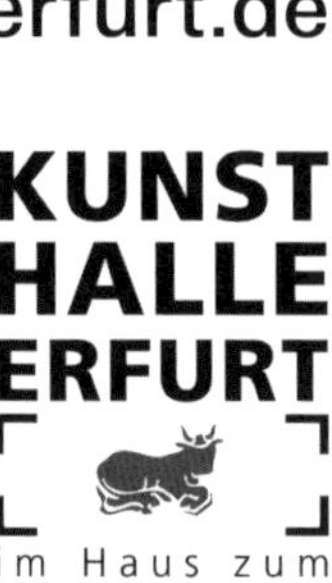

Übersetzung|Translation:
Jennifer Taylor

Grafische Gestaltung|
Graphic design: Nora Turato

Reproduktionen|
Reproductions:
Weyhing digital, Ostfildern

Herstellung|Production:
Julia Günther, Hatje Cantz

Papier|Paper:
Olin Smooth High White,
150 g/m^2

Gesamtherstellung|
Printing and binding:
DZA Druckerei zu Altenburg
GmbH, Altenburg

Erschienen im|
Published by
Hatje Cantz Verlag
Zeppelinstrasse 32
73760 Ostfildern
Deutschland|Germany
Tel. +49 711 4405-200
Fax +49 711 4405-220
www.hatjecantz.com
Ein Unternehmen der
Ganske Verlagsgruppe|
A Ganske Publishing
Group company

Hatje Cantz books are
available internationally
at selected bookstores.
For more information about
our distribution partners,
please visit our website at
www.hatjecantz.com.

ISBN 978-3-7757-3820-0

Printed in Germany

Mit freundlicher
Unterstützung von|With
generous support from:

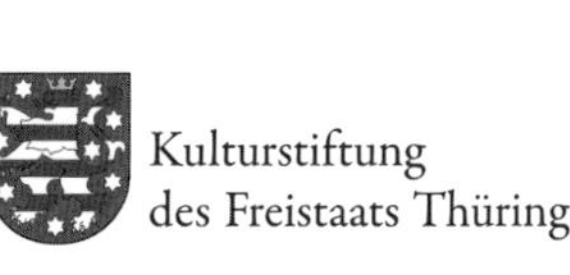

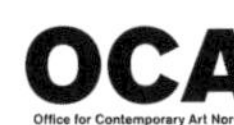